Liberal Arts in the Doldrums

Liberal Arts in the Doldrums

Rethink, Revise, and Revitalize to Reverse the Trend

John J. Hampton

ROWMAN & LITTLEFIELD
Lanham • Boulder • New York • London

Published by Rowman & Littlefield
A wholly owned subsidiary of The Rowman & Littlefield Publishing Group, Inc.
4501 Forbes Boulevard, Suite 200, Lanham, Maryland 20706
www.rowman.com

Unit A, Whitacre Mews, 26-34 Stannary Street, London SE11 4AB

British Library Cataloguing in Publication Information Available

Library of Congress Cataloging-in-Publication Data

Names: Hampton, John J., 1942- author.
Title: Liberal arts in the doldrums : rethink, revise, and revitalize to reverse the trend / John J. Hampton.
Description: Lanham, Maryland : Roman & Littlefield, 2017. | Includes bibliographical references.
Identifiers: LCCN 2017016295| ISBN 9781475837957 (cloth : alk. paper) | ISBN 9781475837964 (pbk. : alk. paper)
Subjects: LCSH: Education, Humanistic—United States. | Education, Higher—Aims and objectives—United States. | Education, Higher—Curricula—United States. | Educational change—United States.
Classification: LCC LC1023 .H36 2017 | DDC 370.11/2—dc23 LC record available at https://lccn.loc.gov/2017016295

∞™ The paper used in this publication meets the minimum requirements of American National Standard for Information Sciences—Permanence of Paper for Printed Library Materials, ANSI/NISO Z39.48-1992.

Printed in the United States of America

Contents

PART III: REVISING THE PROFESSORIATE

PART IV: RESTRUCTURING THE CURRICULUM

PART V: REACHING BEYOND THE CLASSROOM

Preface

WELCOME TO THE ACADEMY

In modern usage, the term "academy" has three common meanings:

- **Training Institution.** A place to study prior to entering a special field. An example is a police academy.
- **Educational Institution.** Synonyms are school, college, university, institute, seminary, and conservatory.
- **Society or Institution.** Distinguished scholars, artists, or scientists accomplished in a particular field.

The usage of the term academy in this book is narrow. It refers to:

> A college or university that offers a bachelor's degree built upon a liberal arts foundation.

Plato may be dead now for twenty-four hundred years, but his ideal is alive today across North America and elsewhere.

PREMISES OF THIS BOOK

The premises are two-fold:

- **Value of the Liberal Arts.** When presented in the right format, the breadth of the liberal arts shows us how to use critical thinking to make timely and accurate decisions about important things in our lives.

- **Reform Needed.** The liberal arts are being undermined in many of today's colleges and universities.

We will address reforms to modernize the liberal arts in the United States and Canada. By implication, our effort contains lessons useful around the world.

ESCALATOR SPEECH (THIRTY SECONDS)

The liberal arts are the foundation for a successful adult life. Unfortunately, they are lost in a time warp in many institutions. The goal is to create an educated person, but the mechanisms to achieve the goal are brittle. We argue for changes to the professoriate, restructuring of the liberal arts curriculum, and taking a new perspective to breathe fresh air into the undergraduate experience.

ELEVATOR SPEECH (SIXTY SECONDS)

This book argues for changes in the common cultural heritage of an educated person. It addresses the need to differentiate teaching and scholarship. It proposes expansive views of an undergraduate education. It explains why colleges and universities must replace parochialism, reform the public perception of higher education, revise the professoriate, restructure the liberal arts curriculum, and extend the lessons of the liberal arts beyond the classroom.

SPECIFIC RECOMMENDATIONS

- **Replace Parochialism in the Liberal Arts.** Broaden the perspective of critical thinking and how it creates an educated person.
- **Reform the Public Perception of Higher Education.** People need a clearer understanding of what's going on.
- **Revise the Professoriate.** Create separate career paths to differentiate talented teachers and scholars.
- **Restructure Curriculum.** Change the context of courses to pursue outcomes, not disciplines.
- **Reach Beyond the Classroom.** Take students beyond knowledge into behavior.

LESSONS FROM THE LIBERAL ARTS

We address probing questions affecting higher education today:

- What do we mean when we say someone has a "liberal arts" education?
- Is it wartime or peacetime for colleges today?
- Are colleges preparing students for real-world problem solving?
- Are attacks on higher education resulting from a misunderstanding of what colleges do?
- Are reputation and accreditation good guides to college quality?
- Is it the job of professors to interpret the truth?
- Does higher education reward excellent teachers?
- Do college professors deserve greater recognition and respect?
- Do the liberal arts improve decision making?
- Do the liberal arts prepare students for employment after college?
- What areas and tools for decision making are missing in liberal arts curricula?
- What challenges to the liberal arts are being ignored today?

COMPARISON OF THE THREE BOOKS

This is third of three books that frame current issues in higher education around the professoriate and liberal arts curriculum. Conditions are described. Behaviors are analyzed. Strengths and weaknesses are examined. Changes are recommended.

The following descriptions offer a side-by-side comparison.

CULTURE, INTRICACIES, AND OBSESSIONS: WHY COLLEGES AND UNIVERSITIES ARE STRUGGLING TO DELIVER THE GOODS

This book opens the door of the faculty lounge and takes the reader into colleges and universities as seen from the viewpoint of an insider. It explains why students are being shortchanged in terms of developing character and useful life lessons. It identifies problems and recommends major changes to restore confidence in higher education.

THE PROFESSORIATE TODAY—LANGUISHING IN DANTE'S PURGATORY

The changing role and expectations of higher education have reached a crisis point. The heart of the problem is an isolation of the professoriate. An emphasis on obscure research and lack of accountability is undermining the academy. Current approaches to writing a doctoral dissertation and pursuing tenure and promotion border on the absurd. They produce a period of suffering for new professors quite comparable to the description of purgatory in Dante's *Divine Comedy*. This book documents the story.

LIBERAL ARTS IN THE DOLDRUMS: LET'S FIX IT!

The liberal arts are lost in a time warp in many institutions. The goal is to create an educated person, but the mechanisms to achieve the goal are brittle. This book argues for changes to the professoriate, restructuring of the liberal arts curriculum, and taking a new perspective to breathe fresh air into the undergraduate environment.

FULL DISCLOSURE

The author is a professor at a liberal arts university. He and his colleagues in business administration and education engage students who have a liberal arts foundation. What the students get out of it seems to be based largely on the professors they select and the energy they expend on learning.

We think business administration courses pursue the same outcomes as the liberal arts core. This includes improving critical thinking and decision making, building ethical and moral values, and shaping skills so graduates can lead lives as productive and decent citizens. Thus, the liberal arts foundation is strengthened in upper-division business courses. We know our colleagues in elementary and secondary school education feel the same way.

The arguments in this book supporting reforms in the liberal arts apply also to undergraduate business and education disciplines.

ACKNOWLEDGMENTS

So many people shaped this treatise. Malcolm Gladwell is at the top of the list. Others are colleagues at Saint Peter's; Professors Elaine Ognibene and

Richard Ognibene, both formerly of Siena College; and Kevin Birmingham, James Lang, and Nicholas Lemann, currently writing on higher education. Thanks also to the *Chronicle of Higher Education*, whose daily electronic missives bring new insights into the daily opening of email software.

John J. Hampton
Litchfield, Connecticut
April 2017

Part I

REPLACING PAROCHIALISM IN THE LIBERAL ARTS

Chapter One

What's the Difference between Believing and Knowing? Is Your Truth Everybody's Truth?

Everything we see is a perspective, not the truth.

—attributed to Marcus Aurelius, Roman emperor

WHAT DOES AN ELEPHANT LOOK LIKE?

An ancient story from India tells of six blind men who were asked to describe an elephant by feeling different parts of the elephant's body. One man touched a leg and described a pillar. The man who touched a tusk had a different description, and so did the men who felt the tail, trunk, belly, and ear. The story is often used to demonstrate the possibility of different forms of truth depending upon one's perspective or lack thereof.

In many ways, this story encapsulates the journey that is about to begin.

QUESTION

Are the following messages advertising cigarettes in the 1950s true?

- Newport refreshes while you smoke.
- Your taste buds will tell you why you'll feel better about smoking with the taste of Kent.
- Should a gentleman offer a Tiparillo to a librarian?
- Pall Mall's natural mildness is so good to your taste.

ANSWER

Maybe. We need to ask very old smokers if they are still alive.

QUESTION

Are these messages advertising for cigarettes in the 1970s true?

- Kool Super Lights, A most refreshing low "tar."
- Virginia Slims. You've come a long way, baby.
- Benson & Hedges 100s. I was trying to be sophisticated and then it happened.

ANSWER

Maybe. We need to ask old smokers. Some should still be alive.

QUESTION

In-between the 1950s and 1970s, the federal government required warnings about the danger of smoking to be placed on every pack of cigarettes. Is the following 1964 warning true?

> SURGEON GENERAL'S WARNING: Smoking Causes Lung Cancer, Heart Disease, Emphysema, and May Complicate Pregnancy.

ANSWER

A lot of evidence supports the statement. In the 1950s, half of adult men over the age of seventeen were smokers. The applicable number for women was 30 percent. Many would later develop lung cancer or other diseases.

QUESTION

In 1994, Congress subpoenaed the top executives of the seven largest U.S. tobacco companies and asked them to testify under oath whether they believed nicotine to be addictive. Every single one testified that they believed nicotine was not addictive. The Department of Justice accused the executives of perjury. Could it be proven under the law?

ANSWER

Probably not. Charges were never filed because of the careful wording of the statements. Each executive said, "I believe that nicotine is not addictive." A belief is a matter of personal opinion rather than objective fact.

OUR BELIEFS

The Great Wall of China is the only man-made object visible from the moon. How do I know that? I have always known it. Trust me. It's true.

What else do I believe? Lots of things. We all do. Try this yourself. Take the following test. Compare your results with the answers that follow the last question.

1. Which of the following was ranked highest in overall quality by J. D. Powers in 2016 for large passenger cars?
   A. Toyota — C. Chevrolet
   B. Mercedes — D. Hyundai
2. Which of the following has the most retail outlets in the world?
   A. McDonald's — C. Dunkin' Donuts
   B. Subway — D. Kentucky Fried Chicken
3. What is the color of the box that can survive the crash of a commercial airliner and provide data on what happened?
   A. Red — C. Black
   B. White — D. None of the above
4. Which of the following countries has the largest volume of proven oil reserves?
   A. Saudi Arabia — C. Canada
   B. Venezuela — D. None of the above
5. Which of the following is the best-selling beer in the world?
   A. Heineken — C. Budweiser
   B. Snow — D. None of the above
6. How many bodily senses do we have (such as hearing, smell, and taste)?
   A. Five
   B. Six
   C. Seven
   D. More than seven

7. Which of the following is the reason Saint Bernard rescue dogs carry liquor in a cask around their neck for stranded hikers or fallen skiers in snow?
   A. Alcohol warms the body
   B. Alcohol stimulates nerves
   C. Alcohol stimulates blood flow
   D. None of the above
8. Which of the following are warriors in ancient times who wore helmets with horns on them?
   A. Vikings C. Mongols
   B. Goths D. None of the above
9. Which of the following does not grow on a tree?
   A. Bananas C. Avocados
   B. Cashews D. All grow on trees
10. Which of the following categories contains tomatoes?
   A. Vegetables C. Fruits
   B. Flowers D. None of the above

ANSWERS TO WIDELY KNOWN BELIEFS

Before we start, the Great Wall of China is not the only man-made object visible from the Moon. No man-made object is visible. Our other misconceptions:

1. Highest in overall quality. **Hyundai.**
2. Most retail outlets. **Subway.**
3. Color of box that survives plane crash. **Orange, which is so easily visible in water.**
4. Largest proven oil reserves. **Venezuela.**
5. Best-selling beer. **Snow (China).**
6. Bodily senses. **A total of thirteen.**
7. Saint Bernard dogs and liquor. **None. Liquor drops the body temperature. The keg comes from an ad campaign for Switzerland.**
8. Warriors with horns on helmets. **None.**
9. Does not grow on tree. **Bananas.**
10. Tomatoes are: **Fruits.**

How did you do? For your information, the above test has been administered to a long list of family, friends, and colleagues. The average score is three correct answers. The confidence expressed by the participants is much higher. Before seeing the answers, most test takers express strong confidence that they had seven or more correct answers.

QUESTION

How many of the world's five tallest buildings are in the United States? If someone offers you a bet on getting the right answer, would you put up $100 to win $500 with the right answer?

ANSWER

Answer is ahead.

QUESTION

A person offers you another bet. He has a piece of paper with a dictionary definition of the word "sewer." You win one hundred dollars if you match any word on the paper. Would you take the bet?

ANSWER

Answer is ahead.

RMS *TITANIC*

Decision making occurs when we apply a belief to a specific situation. Sometimes we get it right. Other times we have a disaster. It was not much different more than one hundred years ago. We can remind ourselves of the words of Captain Edward Smith when he was commander of the RMS *Adriatic* in 1907:

> I cannot imagine any condition which would cause a ship to founder. I cannot conceive of any vital disaster happening to this vessel. Modern ship building has gone beyond that.

Five years later, he was the first and only commander of the RMS *Titanic*. In an interview, he said:

> We do not care anything for the heaviest storms in these big ships. It is fog that we fear. The big icebergs. . . . If a vessel should run on one of these, half her bottom might be torn away.

Finally, a likely conversation between a White Star Line executive and Captain Smith in the early evening of April 14, 1912:

> **White Star Executive:** "Full steam ahead for the Royal Mail Ship *Titanic*, Captain Smith. We must set a record for a transatlantic crossing."
> **Captain Smith:** Reply unknown.

Captain Smith steamed at full speed into a field of icebergs on a foggy night. It was not an unforeseeable accident. It occurred when an experienced captain made a bad decision.

Why does this happen? How can we tempt icebergs, even as we sail on the mightiest ship ever built? Why do we ignore warnings? Why do we sometimes make such judgments and decisions?

CRITICAL THINKING

A starting point to answer this question is introduce a concept. Critical thinking occurs when we make clear, reasoned judgments based on available information. The thinker skillfully analyzes, assesses, and reconstructs an idea, event, or situation and draws an accurate picture about its meaning. To improve critical thinking, we must learn to observe, reflect, and communicate. Then, we use reasoning, experimentation, and past experience to draw conclusions. Upon them, we take decisions and actions.

Critical thinking leads us to the question, "How do people make decisions?" To help us, here are a few definitions:

- **Facts.** Empirical data or observable phenomenon supported by evidence.
- **Beliefs.** Combination of facts and interpretations of people and activities.
- **Feelings.** Emotional state or reactions to the world around us.
- **Opinions.** Judgments without knowing the source of the viewpoint.
- **Assumptions.** Conclusions without reflection.
- **Bias.** A prejudgment that interferes with an objective perspective.

QUESTION

A professor asked a class of twenty undergraduate students to identify people's primary approach to decision making. The choices were facts, beliefs, feelings, opinions, assumptions, and judgment. Which one received the most votes?

ANSWER

This experiment, which has been done countless times, produces a wide array of responses. Most students choose between facts and beliefs, but feelings, opinions, and assumptions are not too far behind. Occasionally, bias will receive a vote.

ANSWER TO FIVE TALLEST BUILDINGS

In 2017, none were in the United States. The countries were Dubai, Taipei, Shanghai, Hong Kong, and Kuala Lumpur.

ANSWER TO DEFINITION OF "SEWER"

Someone who sews.

BELIEFS IN CRITICAL THINKING

Considerable research, as well as common sense, supports the reality that beliefs form the basis for decisions and actions. Think about it. People either ignore facts or select them to support their beliefs. Facts give us:

- A basis for reaching a decision.
- A need to reach a decision.
- An excuse to reach a decision.
- A way to defend the wrong decision.

Feelings and assumptions are not much help. They distort decisions. Feelings intensify or diminish facts and beliefs. Assumptions are beliefs without reflection.

Opinions and bias are even more dangerous. They overwhelm our beliefs. We mask opinions as facts. Bias creates a preference for irrational conclusions

Thus, we arrive at a recognition that beliefs are the basis for the decisions we make. It is that simple. To improve critical thinking, we must improve how we form our beliefs.

QUESTION

Vimal Patel, a journalist from the *Chronicle of Higher Education*, took a long bus trip to the 2016 presidential inauguration. He rode with Indiana State University students and staff members to Washington, District of Columbia.

Prior to the trip, he asked a conservative male student to connect him with a Trump supporter who had never been outside Indiana. The student responded with an accusation that the journalist was stereotyping Trump supporters and he was "not going to try to find someone who fits your story to get you a raise for pushing biased information." Is it likely that this young man has a liberal arts education?

ANSWER

Maybe not. Would the student recognize the irony of denouncing stereotyping while he himself engages in stereotyping? Does the student recognize his own immaturity of drawing conclusions on motives based upon a biased assumption?

QUESTION

When everyone boarded the bus, the journalist took a seat next to the student. He told the student he made the same inquiry to Democrats as part of a story about people participating in politics. The atmosphere abruptly changed, and the journalist and student "chatted warmly" during the ride. The student said he misunderstood, apologized, and introduced Patel to a Trump supporter who became part of the published story.

NEW ORLEANS AND KATRINA

Everybody knew that New Orleans flooded. It happened every three years since the levees were first built. Usually it was caused by rain and the flooding subsided in a few days or weeks. Naturally, the city's leaders had concerns. They had to take care of the biggest problem. What should they do with people who died?

It was not good to put bodies in the ground. After a flood, the muddy earth would release its treasures. Caskets would float down the streets. Nor did the city want cemeteries on the limited amount of high ground where the prosperous citizens had homes. No powerful person wanted a cemetery next to a fine home. Not in my neighborhood.

The solution came after a particularly bad Mississippi River flood in 1789. The city decided to build tombs above ground. A seven-foot interior slab at the top of a brick and plaster structure would hold the dearly departed. By law, the tomb could not be opened for a year after being sealed with a body. The New Orleans summer would raise inside temperatures to 350 degrees Fahrenheit. When the tomb was reopened to allow the "burial" of another family member, only ashes would remain to be swept aside.

What if two people died in a close time proximity and the family wanted them together for eternity? One body would wait patiently in a holding area and be placed in the tomb after a year.

QUESTION

What does the story of Hurricane Katrina have to do with facts and beliefs?

ANSWER

It is an example of a belief trumping a fact. The belief was that the problem with flooding had been addressed. The fact is that the levees were in danger. They were not built to withstand hurricanes that were becoming stronger with rising temperatures. The historically strong Katrina killed fifteen hundred residents of the city.

QUESTION

Reflections upon New Orleans lead us to a question. Should we expect a liberal arts education to help students use facts to make better decisions before they face bad consequences as adults?

ANSWER

Most people say yes. Teenagers tend to be confident that they make good decisions. To develop personal independence, they challenge and resist parents, teachers, and friends who try to tell them what to do. In many cases, they don't get it right. College should help.

CLICHÉS

One place where the liberal arts can really help involves actions without reflection. It is only a short walk from beliefs to clichés. Students and everyone else uses them all the time to support their beliefs. They are both common and useful but they pose problems:

- **Past Orientation.** They reflect experiences that may no longer be valid.
- **Change Resistant.** They confirm a continuation of the past without real reflection.
- **Little Creativity.** They discourage new ideas.

Truth matters. It really does. The place to understand truth is in a liberal arts environment. Not in a series of courses randomly strung together. These reflect the power of individual professors or academic departments. Instead, colleges and universities should help students distinguish among beliefs, facts, assumptions, opinions, and bias. Then, augment critical thinking by recognizing motivations, emotions, and capabilities. This total package creates the ability for young people to discover themselves and the opportunities that await them.

That's the big picture. We cannot change it. We can do more to help shape it.

CONCLUSION AND FALLACIES

Many things get in the way of our efforts to understand what's happening. Past beliefs shape our conclusions and actions. In many ways, education is a search for the truth so our beliefs are correct. Hence:

Fallacy 1. People have their beliefs and that is their right.
Reality 1. An educated person does not allow belief to overcome evidence.

Chapter Two

Are We Fighting a Decline in Critical Thinking? Is "Truthiness" Really a Word in the Dictionary?

NOT CRITICAL THINKING

At a school reunion, a philosophy professor met an alumnus. The two were talking:

Alumnus: What do you teach?
Professor: I teach logic.
Alumnus: What do you mean?
Professor: Let me give you an example. Do you have a dog?
Alumnus: Yes.
Professor: Probably for your children.
Alumnus: Yes.
Professor: That means you must be married.
Alumnus: Yes.
Professor: Thus, I devised the fact that you are heterosexual.
Alumnus: Wow.
Professor: That's how you do critical thinking.

QUESTION

A few days after talking to the professor, the alumnus met a stranger at a business conference. He decided to show off his new understanding of logic.

Alumnus: I just learned about logic.
Stranger: What do you mean?
Alumnus: I'll show you. Do you have a dog?
Stranger: No.

Alumnus: That tells me something about you.
Stranger: What is that?
Alumnus: You do not have a dog. That means you must be gay.

QUESTION

Professor Rob Jenkins from Georgia State describes his classes with educators who teach kindergarten to college. He asks, "How can we help young people learn?" What happens?

ANSWER

Typically, in a few minutes someone will say, "I know, let's teach critical thinking!" Then, someone will follow with, "Oh, that's good. Write that down." Most people then "nod sagely" and write it down.

Professor Jenkins believes "critical thinking" has become an educational catchphrase overused to the point of having no meaning at all. Do people simply refuse to recognize reality, as with the *Titanic* and Katrina, or are we locked into clichés? The answer is yes to both questions. Our beliefs shape our thinking, help us function, and betray us. Still, there is something else that harms critical thinking. We are fooled by beliefs that are created in childhood. I have a few of those.

CHILDHOOD BELIEFS

Classroom discussions work well when linked to personal experiences. Three of my favorites deal with Grandma, Uncle Pat, and Mrs. Link:

- **Grandma.** She identified herself as a Democrat, Roman Catholic, and atheist.
- **Uncle Pat.** His advice was to be an accountant. His belief was the economic depression of the 1930s would return. America would always need bookkeepers.
- **Mrs. Link.** This high school teacher gave all students the same advice. Get a certification to teach in a public school as a safeguard against unemployment.

BELIEFS OR FACTS?

The beliefs of all three adults could be challenged for a failure of critical thinking:

- Question: "Grandma. How can a person be a Democrat, Catholic, and atheist?"
- Answer: "The Republicans don't care about the little people. Our whole family was born Catholic. No God would allow so many bad things to happen to good people."
- Statement: "Uncle Pat, accounting sounds boring."
- Response: "Ignore that fact. Choose it. You'll make money."
- Statement: "Mrs. Link, I can conquer the world."
- Response: "Maybe yes, maybe no. Get a teaching certificate. You can always get a job."

STETSON UNIVERSITY

Childhood advice can be helpful but it clouds efforts to sort facts from beliefs. When do we grasp the critical difference between reality and a belief? For many of us, this occurs during four college years spent in traditional classrooms. My growth in understanding occurred at Stetson University.

Stetson had an honors program that largely allowed independent work with individual professors. The environment encouraged students to compare what they were told by professors, what they thought they knew, and resolve the inconsistencies therein.

QUESTION

One Stetson memory involved writing a paper contrasting the ideas of two famous professors. The goal was to resolve a complicated disagreement on a single concept. The process required each student to individually discuss the paper with both professors. After forty-five minutes or so, it became clear that a key point of logic was reversed and the paper reached a completely wrong conclusion. Did the mistake produce a failing grade for the course?

ANSWER

No. Exactly the opposite happened. The professors treated engagement in critical thinking as a positive. The paper and interaction with mentors produced learning in the tradition of Plato and the medieval university. Critical thinking was alive in the academy.

A WELL-CULTIVATED CRITICAL THINKER

What can we expect from a liberal arts education? Maybe:

- **Analysis.** Can students identify purpose? Why are we asking a question or seeking an answer to a question? What information do we need and what inferences, assumptions, implications, and beliefs shape the discussion?
- **Self-Introspection.** Can students assess the quality of their own reasoning? Is it characterized by clarity, accuracy, precision, and relevance? Does it pursue depth and breadth? Does it reach conclusions that are significant and logical?

CRITICAL THINKING

If education improves critical thinking, it shows students how to raise vital questions, identify important problems, and attack answers and solutions:

- Formulate the issue clearly and precisely.
- Gather and assess relevant information.
- Use abstract ideas.
- Consider assumptions, implications, and consequences of alternative strategies.
- Communicate effectively with others to test ideas and consider alternative systems of thought.
- Draw well-reasoned conclusions and propose workable solutions.

QUESTION

Taylor Swift, the popular and wealthy contemporary female recording artist, takes her two cats, Meredith and Olivia, with her on a private jet. If this country experienced a shortage of milk, Ms. Swift might buy milk for her cats that otherwise is needed by poor mothers to help their children avoid rickets.

Is it fair and ethical that our economic system allows the rich to buy anything while others can become ill or die?

ANSWER

Ask this question to students who completed Economics 101. You can judge for yourself how well we are doing with developing critical thinking in college. If the answer makes no sense, why do we care if the student can explain the theory of the competitive market model of economics?

DECLINE IN CRITICAL THINKING

Professor Tom Nichols of the U.S. Naval War College argues that colleges are undermining critical thinking. He identifies the problem as stemming from pampering students as customers, a proliferation of "faux universities," grade inflation, and a power reversal between instructor and student. The decline in critical thinking produces citizens unprepared for their duties. College graduates join lesser-educated residents in the confusion that arises from "indifferent and lazy grazing of cable, talk radio, and the web" (Tom Nichols, "Our Graduates Are Rubes," *Chronicle of Higher Education*, January 15, 2017). The result is "relentless conflict on social media, taking offense at everything while believing anything."

POST-TRUTH AND TRUTHINESS

The Oxford and Merriam-Webster dictionaries of English are authoritative sources on the current usage of English words. They both recognize the decline in critical thinking about "truth."

- ***Truthiness.*** This noun refers to a truth that won't allow itself to be held back by evidence. We know it intuitively "from the gut" or because it "feels right." We completely ignore logic, intellectual examination, or contradictory evidence.
- ***Post-truth.*** This adjective describes appeals to emotion and personal beliefs that shape public opinion despite sharply conflicting and largely accurate facts. Evidence is ignored as a message is accepted and repeated.

The two words are relatively new in the English language. *Truthiness* was coined and popularized by American comedian Stephen Colbert in 2005. He applied it to the U.S. decision to invade Iraq in 2003. *Post-truth* dates back more than thirty years. It got a boost in *The Post-Truth Era*, a book that appeared in 2004. The word's usage spiked in frequency in 2016 in the context of the United Kingdom vote to leave the European Union and the U.S. presidential election.

QUESTION

With respect to many social media messages accepted by college students and others, is "post-truth" or "truthiness" a better word to describe what's happening?

ANSWER

Even experts do not agree. In 2006, Merriam-Webster chose "truthiness" as its word of the year. Oxford Dictionary picked "post-truth" as its word of the year in 2016.

QUESTION

Is the debate between "truthiness" and "post-truth" the end of the story of critical thinking weakness?

ANSWER

Probably not. Stephen Colbert updated his world vision by introducing "trumpiness" in 2016. Much as science marches forward, Colbert explained that truthiness refers to statements that "feel" true but are actually false. "Trumpiness" does not even have to feel true, much less be true.

2016 PRESIDENTIAL ELECTION

At this point, most readers may suspect the above discussion reflects partisan politics. Republicans may hate it. Democrats may think it is spot on. Independents may wonder why it does not present a balanced viewpoint.

It does actually. Both political parties engaged in truthiness. Hillary Clinton and Donald Trump campaigned actively recognizing that voting decisions are made based on beliefs. The candidates often played with the facts. PolitiFact.com, a project operated by the *Tampa Bay Times*, checks the "facts" in statements by members of Congress, the White House, lobbyists, and interest groups. In the 2016 election campaign, they graded the statements of the Democratic and Republican nominees as follows:

	Number	*Percent*
Hillary Clinton		
True	72	25
Mostly true	76	26
Half true	69	24
Mostly false	40	14
Pants on fire	7	2
Total	293	100
Donald Trump		
True	14	4
Mostly true	39	11
Half true	51	15
Mostly false	63	18
False	114	33
Total	343	100

BELIEFS AND BETRAYAL

For many reasons, our beliefs betray us. It might be the result of cigarette ads, political statements, or a variety of other messages, situations, or experiences. Developed in childhood and modified by human tendencies, our beliefs lead us to wait too long to make changes that improve our lives. We rely on outdated assumptions and opinions. We ignore facts. We fail to understand our emotions and biases.

We can do better. We can fix things before they break. We can spot conditions that affect our world positively and negatively and respond to them. We may think the liberal arts helps students understand the truth. It is not entirely clear that this means the same thing to everyone who believes it.

CONCLUSION AND FALLACIES

Critical thinking moves people in the direction of understanding what is happening. If it undoes the incorrect things we think we know or confirms that which is logical, it is a powerful tool. Hence:

Fallacy 2. The beliefs formed as we grow up allow us to understand the truth.
Reality 2. College should help us separate beliefs from opinions, assumptions, emotions, and bias.

Chapter Three

What Does It Mean to be an Educated Person? Is Everybody Talking the Same Language?

> I know you think you understand what you thought I said but I'm not sure you realize that what you heard is not what I meant.
>
> —attributed to Alan Greenspan, American economist

REFLECTION ON IRRELEVANT COURSE

The trickiest course I ever taught was Money and Banking, a sophomore year panoramic exploration of U.S. monetary and financial systems. It was a required course for business majors. The material was irrelevant to most students.

I was in trouble right from the get-go, trying to differentiate among three different types of money: commodity, fiat, and bank. Honest to God, the students did not care. On graduation day, no one had a clue about the meaning of "fiat money." Some did not know it when they answered the multiple choice question on the midterm exam. A famous quote:

> I hear and I forget. I see and I remember. I do and I understand.
>
> —attributed to Confucius

A less famous quote:

> If I don't care about it when I study it, I forget it no matter what.
>
> —attributed to anonymous college students

SOFT AND HARD LIFE SKILLS

In the bigger picture, why do most students hate money and banking? Could it be that the content of the course contains no useful life skills? Viewed in two categories:

- **Soft Skills.** A combination of interpersonal, social, and communication skills to navigate your personal and professional environment.
- **Hard Skills.** Specific, teachable abilities that can be defined and measured, such as math, using computers, performing carpentry tasks, and calculating personal taxes.

Money and banking, in the minds of most young people, contain theories, concepts, institutions, and economic structures. None of these have relevance to anything going on in their lives.

LIBERAL ARTS TRADITION

From this introduction, we acknowledge the liberal arts. For millennia, the term described subjects and skills essential to take an active part in civic life. A goal of the liberal arts is to broaden life skills, both hard and soft.

The term "liberal" was not used in contrast to "conservative." It comes from the Latin to indicate studies that were "free and unrestricted."

The concept of a liberal arts education traces back to the ancient Greeks and Romans. The academy of Plato sought to produce a person who was virtuous, ethical, knowledgeable in many fields, and capable of participating in public debate.

That effort morphed into a Judeo-Christian framework largely identified with Europe and North America. It is globally renowned for helping students understand the values, ethics, and ideas that created Western civilization. Grounded in philosophy and religion, it went through phases:

- **Pre-Christian Concepts.** Notable names were Socrates (b. 470 BC), Plato, (b. 428 BC), and Aristotle (b. 384 BC).
- **Early Christian Theologians.** Here we find Paul of Tarsus (b. 5 BC), Augustine of Hippo (b. 354 AD), and Thomas Aquinas (b. 1225 AD).
- **Renaissance Philosophers.** Many names arise here, including Rene Descartes (b. 1596), John Locke (b. 1632), Isaac Newton (b. 1642), and Immanuel Kant (b. 1724).

QUESTION

What were the subjects and skills that made up the liberal arts in ancient Greece?

ANSWER

The foundation topics covered grammar, logic, and rhetoric, augmented by arithmetic, geometry, music, and astronomy.

LIBERAL ARTS TODAY

In modern times, a liberal arts education can be interpreted in two primary ways.

- **Academic Subjects.** These include literature, philosophy, mathematics, and social and physical sciences.
- **Academic Program.** Alternatively, it can describe a complete degree program in a liberal arts area.

For both interpretations, the term generally excludes professional and vocational courses and degrees.

SPECTRUM OF GENERAL EDUCATION

The first two years of college generally cover a common cultural heritage in a liberal arts framework. Professors agree on the concept but disagree on its contents. Most colleges and universities accept the liberal arts spectrum as containing four fields:

- **Humanities.** Includes art, literature, philosophy, religion, ethics, languages, music, theater, and speech.
- **Social Sciences.** Such as history, geography, psychology, sociology, political science, and economics.
- **Natural Sciences.** Examples are biology, chemistry, physics, and earth science.
- **Formal Sciences.** A grouping that includes logic, mathematics, statistics, and computer science.

When defining a general education, disagreement among professors often reflects narrow perspectives. They value their own discipline and seek to get the courses they teach included among the requirements.

Administrators and other parties influence general education discussions. A college aligned with a religious body might include multiple philosophy and theology courses. A state university has public service issues to consider for taxpayers. A private secular institution might incorporate additional social responsibility or community service courses.

Business and education degrees are commonly built upon a liberal arts foundation. The same may be true for science or engineering. All students may take the same first two years of full-time study. This approach often produces five-year bachelor's degree programs.

QUESTION

A history professor believes two history courses should be required of all undergraduates. An economics professor argues for separate courses in macro and micro economics. Professors in English, political sciences, mathematics, and biology have the same feelings. They get together to discuss the curriculum. How does it go?

ANSWER

Discussions can get quite heated if all the individuals do not get their way.

NON-LIBERAL ARTS EDUCATION

"Non-liberal arts" is an amorphous term that can be applied to undergraduate programs with a vocational orientation. Use of the term riles professors, other educators, college administrators, politicians, and most other parties interested in higher education. It implies a failure to properly educate students as compared to those who choose the liberal arts. Broad classifications of a non-liberal arts education:

- **STEM Degrees.** Academic degrees in science, technology, engineering, and mathematics (aka STEM). STEM schools and degrees prepare students with analytical and technological skills.

- **Career-Oriented Degrees.** Degrees that apply concepts and practices in a specific area of desired future occupation. Examples are education, business, nursing, architecture, and health care management.
- **Vocational Degrees.** Non-academic degrees that lead directly to narrow and specialized careers often offered as two-year or shorter programs. Examples are automotive technology, computer-aided design, residential or commercial electrician, heating, ventilation, air conditioning and refrigeration, dental or medical assisting, and practical nursing.

THE MEANING OF EDUCATION

To understand the controversy over the liberal arts, we can ask, "What does it mean to educate someone?" Education can describe traditional classroom efforts, training by supervised practice in a trade or profession, or other efforts to develop mental, moral, or aesthetic capabilities.

Who does the teaching? The term "academic" can describe everything from a full-time faculty member at a college to a theoretical researcher engaged in scholarly pursuits. The teacher in college may have many titles. The most common:

- **Adjunct.** This is a part-time instructor.
- **Instructor.** A teacher with a master's degree.
- **Assistant Professor.** A junior rank for a teacher usually after obtaining a doctoral degree.
- **Associate Professor.** A middle-level rank usually obtained with some scholarship to augment effective teaching.
- **Professor.** A senior rank often described in conversation as "full professor."

THE EDUCATED PERSON

The interaction between academic and student creates the educated person. Going back to Plato, the educated person is an individual who understands the values, ethics, and ideas that created Western civilization. The term includes two aspects:

- **Concepts.** An understanding of theories, abstract ideas, general notions, beliefs, values, ethics, and morality.
- **Training.** An ability to continue learning because the knowledge, skills, and attitudes developed in college enhance the performance of graduates after they graduate.

QUESTION

So, what is an educated person?

ANSWER

Someone who can deal as an adult in the realm of ideas, engage the world as a productive citizen, and produce a successful life whatever his or her interests.

CHARACTERISTICS OF AN EDUCATED PERSON

We have some agreement on how to identify an educated person.

General characteristics:

- Has been educated holistically: creatively, culturally, spiritually, morally, physically, technologically, and intellectually
- Has a good overview of the natural and social sciences, history and geography, literature, philosophy, and theology
- Appreciates art, music, architecture, and creative genius
- Has specialized knowledge in a particular field

Behavioral characteristics:

- Communicates orally and in writing, clearly and concisely
- Reasons analytically and critically, inductively, and deductively
- Can use mathematics to solve problems
- Challenges assumptions and can discern truth from error
- Distinguishes between relevant and irrelevant information
- Can conceptualize and solve problems
- Makes sound financial decisions
- Pursues lifelong learning

Interpersonal characteristics:

- Understands human nature and establishes lasting relationships
- Cooperates and collaborates effectively with others
- Understands and manages his or her own emotions
- Holds people in equal esteem without regard to gender, race, religion, or ethic origin

- Can identify harmful behaviors, modify them, and admit it when he or she is wrong

LIBERAL ARTS FOUNDATION

Many people agree that the liberal arts encourage a student to develop into an educated person:

- **Broad Preparation.** The breadth of coverage gives students a wide range of opportunity after graduation.
- **Career Choices and Changes.** The wide range of knowledge facilitates job selection and switching careers if a mistake is initially made.
- **Employer Preference.** Chief executive officers and others regularly report a desire to hire liberal arts graduates because they have transferable skills to adapt to a changing workplace.
- **Graduate Study Foundation.** The liberal arts are a strong foundation for pursuing a master's degree.
- **Community Service.** Liberal arts provide a broad perspective to work as a productive member of the community.

QUESTION

What characteristics of today's liberal arts impede the development of an educated person?

ANSWER

It may be argued that the general education foundation of many schools does not achieve the liberal arts goals. Criticisms:

- **Large Lecture Halls.** Do students need to listen, not talk, until they understand an area of study?
- **Prerequisites Gone Mad.** Accounting may be a necessary foundation for finance, but most prerequisites are simply pathways to get rid of things no one wants to study so you can get to the substantive material in your declared major.
- **Seven Types of Intelligence.** Modern research shows intelligence categories of verbal, visual, physical, musical, mathematical, logical, and

interpersonal. If students don't have an aptitude for a liberal arts subject, studying it is a waste of time.

- **Narrow Preparation for the Professor.** Too many teachers know their subject matter and consider their job done if students "parrot" it back. They do not know how to extend it to critical thinking and learning.
- **Professors and Graduate Assistants who don't Care.** In large lecture halls, research professors can't interact one-on-one. Nor do they want to. Graduate assistants are not interested in teaching. It's not why they're in graduate school.

LIBERAL ARTS PAROCHIALISM

When people speak of a liberal arts education, they inadvertently think of a major in a liberal arts discipline. History, psychology, English. That is simply not accurate. It is usually true for students majoring in education, business, and other disciplines at schools with a general education core.

QUESTION

Five individuals are talking a few weeks after graduating from bachelor's degree programs with a general education requirement. One each majored in English literature, Spanish, elementary education, business administration, and mathematics. Which one is most likely to be capable and flexible in a discussion of resolving conflict among nations?

ANSWER

The education major who studied handling children's misbehavior and the business administration major who had human relations may have the most preparation for conflict resolution.

EDUCATION OR VOCATION?

From this foundation, we have both agreement and disagreement:

- **Agreement.** Vocational degree students may achieve few of the benefits of a liberal arts education. The education is valuable but students depend upon high school, reading, and life experience to provide the concepts that colleges offer in the liberal arts.

- **Disagreement.** Some proponents of the liberal arts believe business administration, education, and other career-oriented degrees are vocational programs. As already argued, this is simply not true. Many lessons of the liberal arts are incorporated in the upper-division courses of non-liberal arts degrees.

DEBUNKING MYTHS ABOUT THE LIBERAL ARTS

Sometimes rhetoric overcomes logic. Following are some beliefs about a liberal arts degree. Each one is accompanied by a reality check.

- **Belief.** A student must major in the liberal arts to get a wide-ranging education.
- **Reality.** Business, education, and English literature have the same liberal arts foundation. Does a literature course broaden you the most?
- **Belief.** Career-oriented majors require you to take a majority of your course experience in the major area.
- **Reality.** Not true. Half of your courses are in the liberal arts core. About 25 percent are in the major.
- **Belief.** Liberal arts give you more flexibility to choose a career after college.
- **Reality.** No evidence supports this view.

CONCLUSION AND FALLACIES

Many people with strong views on the role of the liberal arts are quite correct in the value of Plato's Academy and its successor institutions. Still, they should understand that the liberal arts foundation is augmented in many degree programs that pursue further development in critical thinking and values formation. Hence:

Fallacy 3. Liberal arts are a four-year undergraduate degree in a liberal arts discipline.

Reality 3. If done right, liberal arts are a foundation for critical thinking and problem solving.

Part II

REFORMING THE PUBLIC PERCEPTION OF HIGHER EDUCATION

Chapter Four

Is it Peacetime or Wartime in Higher Education? Do We Have to Respond to Attacks on the Liberal Arts?

> Leadership is the art of getting someone else to do something you want done because he wants to do it.
>
> —Dwight D. Eisenhower, military leader and U.S. president

THE UNDERGRADUATE QUANDARY

Undergraduate programs with a liberal arts foundation are preparing people to lead and yet the leadership of so many schools is ignoring attacks that threaten their existence. To quote a former college president:

> The problem is . . . the number of Americans who see the great value of a liberal arts education is dwindling . . . students and their parents still want degrees from prestigious liberal arts colleges, but fewer and fewer value the liberal arts education. . . . In today's market, how is anyone going to get a job as an anthropologist or historian, let alone as a philosopher or expert in [nineteenth]-century English literature? (Scott Jaschik, "Disappearing Liberal Arts Colleges," *Inside Higher Ed*, October 11, 2012)

"RIGOROUS" IS THE KEY

Starting in high school and occasionally earlier, students are primed for college to be a challenging experience.

> "You think this is tough. Wait until you get to college."
> "Professors won't baby you and hold your hand like we do."

High school students are encouraged to take advanced placement courses and achieve good grades. The term "rigorous course load" becomes an axiom for students planning to go to college. Students are challenged to balance the need for rigor with their intellectual limitations, extracurricular interests, family, and friends.

QUESTION

Why does everyone encourage you to pursue a rigorous curriculum in high school?

ANSWER

It gets you in to higher-ranked colleges and is a good predictor of academic success in college. Admissions officers want your transcript to show that you are driven, hard-working, and willing to push yourself.

The urge to be academically rigorous continues in college. Professors warn you about how much work is expected and often encourage work in the absence of much learning. The educational system rewards high grades. Dean's lists and valedictorian recognition are based solely on grade point average. Cooperative experiences and internships tend to be awarded to students with higher grades, as do admissions to graduate schools and offers of employment.

The topic of college workload inspires poets and philosophers. They do not always agree:

- "Success doesn't become reality through magic; it takes sweat, determination, and hard work."
- "If a student hasn't learned it by the time he leaves the classroom, further study is pointless."
- "All things are difficult before they are easy."
- "Too much coursework can cause stress, depression, and even lower grades."
- "I hate studying but good grades control my destiny, so I must put in the work."

LIFE SKILLS AFTER COLLEGE

What is the link between rigorous academic achievement and success after college? In 2014, *U.S. News and World Report* identified the top "soft skills" every college student needs after graduation.

- **Problem Solving.** Determine solutions to problems and resolve issues with no prescribed formula.
- **Leadership.** Demonstrate skills to influence others to achieve goals.
- **Interpersonal Skills.** Effectively carry on a conversation, ask questions, and listen actively.
- **Collaboration.** Function efficiently and appropriately on projects and accept constructive criticism when working with others.
- **Time Management.** Organize work and complete assignments in a timely manner.

QUESTION

Does the liberal arts component of undergraduate education produce at least an understanding of these skills?

ANSWER

If we rank these skills on a scale of one to ten, the role of liberal arts courses might score something like:

Factor	*Score*
Collaboration	1
Interpersonal Skills	2
Problem Solving	7
Time Management	5
Leadership	6

These are not exactly impressive scores. Still, the understanding of problem solving and leadership is significant for those students sufficiently mature to achieve it.

MANAGEMENT OR LEADERSHIP?

Sometime in life, most of us reflect upon behaviors that make people successful. It may come from the great books or conversations with parents, peers, or teachers. It rarely comes from expensive eight hundred-page textbooks. Two broad concepts often emerge:

- **Management.** The ideas, skills, and decisions we make to improve our lives, personal relationships, and organizations where we participate.
- **Leadership.** The concepts, situations, and events that help others improve their lives or achieve their goals.

Unfortunately, our beliefs often fail to distinguish between management and leadership. It is not definitions that matter. Rather, it is the purpose.

- **Management Pursues Stability.** Keep things calm and avoid disruption. We want our schools to be orderly, our homes to be neat, and our lives to be quiet. We manage intensely.
- **Leadership Produces Disruption.** Change the things that are happening today. A new relationship gives us cooperation and conflict. An emerging technology allows us to prosper or lose our job. Pursuit of a new opportunity can take us to exciting places or endanger all we have built thus far.

LEADERSHIP THINKING

We know people can understand risk, assess changing environments, and respond to new conditions. So why do they often fail to react until it is too late? An answer is they often ignore the lessons of leadership.

What qualities distinguish an individual as a leader? Are leaders born or made? We know some individuals display skills early in life, whereas others are first noticed when a great crisis arises. Or is the situation the key to leadership? Do leaders exist because they display behavior in the moment when they are most needed? Partly to answer these questions, we see three styles:

- **Authoritarian.** Dictates goals and strategies and controls activities.
- **Participative.** Describes the goal and encourages others to help achieve it.
- **Laissez-faire.** Allows group members to make the decision.

PEACETIME AND WARTIME LEADERS

A useful approach to leadership recognizes two dominant behaviors.

- **Wartime Leader.** Achieves results when conditions are intense, competition is stiff, and rapid action is needed. Action trumps planning.

- **Peacetime Leader.** Accomplishes the task when accuracy and strategy are the keys to success. The best results depend on creating a strategy, matching resources with a plan, and coordinating the work of others.

QUESTION

Do students exhibit wartime and peacetime behavior when writing a term paper?

ANSWER

Yes, with different goals, behaviors, and planning.

- **Goal.** Wartime is: "I need to get it done." Peacetime asks: "What is the best choice on how to do this?"
- **Behavior.** If wartime, start writing without much advance research. With peacetime, make a list of the sources of information that will be needed.
- **Planning.** When done in wartime, reorganize after writing. When done in peacetime, don't start until satisfied with a detailed table of contents.

QUESTION

A team of students were assigned a group project to write a paper on 9/11. They agreed that one member would do the writing and the others would gather information. They sat around a table with everyone connected to the internet. The writer began working on the computer and made the following statements separated by pausing and typing. Are we witnessing a wartime or peacetime activity?

- "I need a quote on increasing threats of terrorism."
- "I need the name of the airports where the terrorists boarded and the times of departure."
- "I need a quote from the president condemning the attackers."
- "I need some background on Osama bin Laden."
- "I need a quote on what the federal government will do to improve security."

ANSWER

Wartime. A peacetime behavior would gather information first.

QUESTION

Dwight D. Eisenhower was the Supreme Allied Commander in the European Theater in World War II. He led the planning for the Normandy invasion of France in 1944. Was he a wartime or peacetime leader?

ANSWER

Eisenhower was the perfect peacetime leader. He carefully planned the invasion of Normandy involving 325,000 soldiers, fifty-five thousand vehicles, and one hundred thousand tons of supplies. The invasion fleet had seven thousand vessels including twelve hundred warships. Planning took more than one year. Within a month, one million men were landed in France.

QUESTION

George S. Patton was the commander of the Seventh and Third U.S. Armies in the European Theater of World War II. Was he a wartime or peacetime leader?

ANSWER

Patton was a wartime leader. He pushed his troops to drive the enemy out of North Africa. He raced British General Montgomery to capture Messina in Sicily. He led a highly successful and rapid drive across France after Normandy. He relieved trapped troops at Bastogne during the Battle of the Bulge.

QUESTION

When planning was the key, peacetime decision making did the job. When no-nonsense action was needed, a wartime approach was the choice. Of Eisenhower and Patton, who believed "plans are nothing, budgets are nothing, but planning and flexible budgeting are everything?"

ANSWER

Both men believed the same thing. Eisenhower actually verbalized it in a 1957 speech when he said, "Plans are worthless, but planning is everything." The point is individuals may have a propensity to planning or action. Good leaders are sufficiently flexible to consider both.

QUESTION

Why are we discussing wartime and peacetime behavior?

ANSWER

Liberal arts colleges need to do more than help their students become leaders. Many of them desperately need faculty members and administrators who understand wartime and peacetime behavior. Let's be specific.

VIRGINIA INTERMONT COLLEGE

In the years leading up to 2014, all was going well at a school whose web page presented the following picture:

> Virginia Intermont offers a liberal arts education— . . . broad-based learning that cultivates . . . critical thinking, analysis and inquiry. Offering exciting programs and hands-on learning . . . VI is founded on the belief that a broad exposure to knowledge coupled with a nurturing learning environment helps inspire students to pursue their passions.

The college had more than five hundred full-time students and 120 dedicated faculty and staff. It owned eighty horses, and its hallmark program was a major in equine studies. The riding center had two indoor rings, one outdoor ring, four wash stalls, and many turnout paddocks. The barn had just been totally renovated. In 2014, the equestrian team won its seventeenth national championship.

QUESTION

In 2014, was it wartime or peacetime at Virginia Intermont?

ANSWER

Despite all appearances, it was wartime. The college was running out of cash and was several months behind on payroll. Frantic efforts were taking place to survive. They failed. During the 2014 graduation ceremony, the college president announced Virginia Intermont would close its doors after 130 years of operation.

The 2014 graduation took place leaving three hundred students with unfinished programs. Other colleges stepped up to welcome them as transfers. King University agreed to accept 130 years of student records and validate requests for transcripts. The campus was sold in 2016 for $3.3 million.

QUESTION

What on earth could be done with eighty horses and an equine studies program?

ANSWER

Perhaps something, but first let's introduce another school.

EMORY & HENRY COLLEGE

This liberal arts school is seventeen miles up Interstate 81 from the Virginia Intermont riding center. It's mission:

> We affirm the liberal arts as our intellectual foundation and . . . challenge all persons to confront historical and contemporary ideas and . . . develop the ability to think critically about all areas of human experience.

The horses, along with the equestrian program, moved to Emory & Henry College and continued to win competitive events.

QUESTION

In 2014, was it peacetime for Emory & Henry College?

ANSWER

Looks like it. The college had a workable formula for the liberal arts with an outcomes-oriented general education core. All students complete it under the umbrella phrase, "Engaging the Liberal Arts." Students strive to know themselves in terms of beliefs and ethics; connect with others; appreciate the role of service in the community; and explore, experiment, create, and quantify. They pursue a list of proficiencies with thinking, computing, writing, and speaking.

QUESTION

Where does an equine studies major fit into a liberal arts environment?

ANSWER

The outcomes-oriented professional program applies the lessons from the liberal arts foundation. In addition to seven credits while "mounted," students take stable and horse show management, equine nutrition, farrier science, equine health and breeding, and methods of teaching how to ride.

QUESTION

What would students do after completing an equine studies major?

ANSWER

They are prepared for careers in event management as well as activities linked to horses. In the equine world alone, we find horse racing, English and Western riding exhibitions, rodeos and timed events, roping, harness, rough stock competition, and arena sports.

QUESTION

What does the story of Virginia Intermont and Emory & Henry have to do with wartime and peacetime in academia?

ANSWER

It shows the importance of leadership in liberal arts colleges if they are to survive in a changing world. These two prestigious schools were located next door to each other. One responded to new realities. One collapsed despite having a nationally recognized program. Although operating in peacetime in 2014, Emory & Henry had an immediate wartime decision to make. It grabbed the equine studies program and used it to enhance its own offerings with a new and useful outcome.

CONCLUSION AND FALLACIES

The challenge for liberal arts lies in a recognition that colleges and universities are struggling with wartime factors in an environment that traditionally valued peacetime activity. Maybe Plato did not worry about funding and neither did medieval universities supported by the church or modern academies supported by endowments. Many schools today should show a heightened about attacks on the value of college. Hence:

Fallacy 4. We are in peacetime so colleges can respond cautiously to external threats.
Reality 4. For many schools, it is wartime so they need to make reforms before it's too late.

Chapter Five

What's the Big Picture of the Liberal Arts? Where Are We Going?

> Why do you dwell on things that don't matter when there are so many things that do?
>
> —Dennis Sharpe, *Destroyer of Worlds*

LIBERAL ARTS ENCOURAGE ACTION

The liberal arts take us beyond the things that exist today. They build up the forces and factors that shape us and our thinking. They explore ideas, strategies, people, actions, and situations. They effectively incorporate time, decision making, and emotions into judgments. They recognize three times:

- **Past.** What happened? Why did it occur? What were the consequences?
- **Present.** What is the situation today?
- **Future.** What will be the situation in the future if we do nothing?

When we finish college, we should be prepared to recognize the big picture. This means bringing concepts, motivations, behaviors, and causal factors together to understand what is happening and to make correct judgments and reasonable decisions.

QUESTION

A business executive and a liberal arts graduate are discussing improving the volume of business for a hospital. Who is its customer?

ANSWER

Patients need services and come to the facility to receive them. In economic terms, the patient is the customer. An expanded view shows us the customer is rarely the patient. It may be the doctor who has hospital privileges, emergency medical services responder who provides ambulance services, spouse or guardian of a child or aging parent, or the policeman who first arrives on an accident scene.

QUESTION

Who are the customers of the American Red Cross?

ANSWER

It is not the victims of a disaster. They are beneficiaries of rescue operations. The customers, clients really, are the people and organizations that donate funds and support to help restore lives after a disaster, accident, or injury.

QUESTION

Who should be the customers of a hospital or the American Red Cross?

ANSWER

The people or organizations that will need or pay for their services in the future. Current customers may change or may not need the same services as time passes.

QUESTION

We can apply critical thinking lessons to our personal lives. What is the goal of an individual?

ANSWER

Create a life that works. Everything else is an activity to pursue that goal. This goal encourages us to develop attitudes and skills that work successfully with others who, in effect, become our personal customers.

QUESTION

Who is your customer?

ANSWER

It is the person or organization you are trying to satisfy today. It may be a parent, boss, partner, or someone you want to impress.

QUESTION

Who is the customer of a teenager?

ANSWER

It may be a parent, teacher, or guidance counselor who has power over the student. More likely, it is someone in the individual's peer group. It may be a boyfriend or girlfriend, current or former classmate, or leader of a desirable clique of students. A failure to please the "customer" produces bad experiences in high school.

QUESTION

Who should be your customer?

ANSWER

The people or organizations you can serve and thus create a life that works. Only you know your own needs, strengths, and weaknesses. If you need money to be happy, you need a way to make it. If you need attention, you need those who will listen to you. If you need other people to see you as a decent and caring person, you need to help others.

QUESTION

Tom Farrington, a Maryland trial lawyer, was a genius making a closing argument at the end of a trial. Who was his customer?

ANSWER

A jury that had no choice other than to listen to him. He was once asked, "Tom, what is your idea of heaven?" He answered simply, "A big ear." Some professors might have the same feeling.

OUR MISSION IN LIFE

Many people believe they have a mission in life. "I want to raise my children." "I want to build a business." "I am determined to get a book published." These goals and others are all well and good.

The same is true for organizations. Many of them post their mission on the wall for everyone to pass and ignore. Examples are "America's finest amusement park," and "Number One Fun Vacation Spot."

QUESTION

A parent tells a child that his mission in life is to get married and have children. If a mission does nothing for you, should you dedicate yourself to pursue it?

ANSWER

Whatever your answer, the liberal arts foundation encourages you to reflect upon the question.

OUR VISION IN LIFE

Having a vision is different. The big picture encourages visions based on understanding who we are and finding unique opportunities to achieve worthwhile goals. The liberal arts help us look to the future:

- **Keen Insight.** Are we aware of who we are and where we are?
- **Good Judgment.** Do we recognize that change is always a possibility and we can take advantage of new circumstances?
- **Improvement.** Do we approach the future from a personal observation about how to make things better?
- **Imagination.** Does our vision contrast with reality and the "facts"?

A vision of where we are going is much better than a mission to go nowhere.

OUR PURPOSE IN LIFE

Purpose brings together mission and vision. It is a reason to take an action or start a journey. Somewhere in childhood, most of us determine we are valuable. We might also ask whether our life has a purpose. This takes us back to time frames.

- **Present.** What should I do? How should I lead my life?
- **Future.** Where am I going? Why am I trying to get there? Maybe I am studying the wrong subjects. Maybe I need to rethink my priorities and values.
- **Purpose.** What should I be doing? If my current plans do not make sense, should I change my direction?

Or even more simply, the liberal arts may encourage three questions: "What am I doing? What will I be doing? What should I be doing?"

QUESTION

A college student is thinking about what will happen after graduation. Which of the following thoughts is most helpful?

- "Don't pick a job with a lot of vacation time. Pick one that doesn't need escaping from."

- "Remember that you need experience to get a job and you need a job to get experience."
- "You really don't need a career. Just get a job with a big paycheck."
- "Some people want it to happen. Some people wish it would happen. Other people make it happen."
- "Life is too short to work with jerks."
- "Everyone brings joy to the workplace. Some when they join it. Others when they leave."

ANSWER

It varies but one thing is sure. If a student doesn't think about it until graduation, success is likely to be slow.

BILL GATES VISION AND PURPOSE

Bill Gates dropped out of Harvard University in his first year. Did his subsequent behaviors reflect any liberal arts preparation?

- **Startup.** He agreed to provide the operating system for the IBM personal computer when he did not have one to sell. Microsoft was the dominant player in personal computer operations for more than thirty years after its startup.
- **Microsoft Office.** This product slowly deposed competing word processing, spreadsheet, and other applications.
- **Internet and Communications.** This is a separate story. Bill Gates saw an effort was failing and made a dramatic retreat. Let's tell the story.

BILL GATES AND THE INTERNET

In the early 1990s, Microsoft was developing a competing technology against the internet. Bill Gates realized he was losing the battle. Without public discussion, he brought project leaders and software developers into a room and directed everyone to stop the project. Did he have the big picture?

ANSWER

In terms of a big picture, he saw wartime and peacetime clearly.

- **Original Project.** The effort to compete with the internet was peacetime.
- **New Project.** The decisive action to change direction was wartime.

He followed up the meeting with a sixteen-page email canceling all work on the Microsoft system. The wartime decision was followed by a peacetime explanation.

HENRY FORD MODEL T

Henry Ford was manufacturing Model T automobiles in Detroit. Employees worked ten hours a day for six days a week to earn eighteen dollars per week. Such a schedule did not leave time to drive automobiles or do much else. In 1914, Ford changed the nature of work in the United States when he paid workers five dollars a day over a five-day work week. He also shortened the workday to eight hours.

QUESTION

How was Henry Ford's decision the big picture?

ANSWER

Other companies followed. The reduction in working hours, accompanied by a rise in income, increased demand for his vehicles. Sales exploded.

WHY LIBERAL ARTS MATTER

The big picture is not complete without recognizing a simple reality. The United States is a bastion of the liberal arts. Hundreds of colleges and universities use it as a primary description of what they do. Professors, deans, and presidents affirm their allegiance to it. At the same time, not everyone agrees. Roger Zelazny, American poet and author, said, "If the liberal arts do nothing else, they provide engaging metaphors for the thinking they displace." Others agree with the view, "You don't need a liberal arts degree to become well read, a strong mathematician or writer, a leader of others, or a person of high moral values and standards."

Tim Worstall, a Fellow at the Adam Smith Institute in London, asked, "Should we abolish liberal arts degrees?" He points out,

> It's difficult to see anything in English Literature that cannot be learned from books. . . . Drama studies might be rather better studied by going and working as an actor. . . . Who would doubt that modern languages would be better taught by slumming around Europe for four years than by a few hours a week of instruction in an otherwise unilingual environment? (Tim Worstall, "Should We Abolish Liberal Arts Degrees? Quite Possibly, Yes," *Forbes*, September 1, 2012).

CONCLUSION AND FALLACIES

That's enough. Liberal arts matter. Some people disagree with certain aspects of them. The big picture is we need to make updates and improvements. We can find solutions for problems that produce the same or better outcomes than current practices. Hence:

Fallacy 5. The liberal arts separate students from real-world problems.
Reality 5. The big picture encourages professors to use the liberal arts to engage students in better ways of thinking.

Chapter Six

Why Should We Listen to Weak Signals? How Long Can We Ignore the Obvious?

> Politics is the ability to foretell what is going to happen tomorrow, next week, next month and next year, and to have the ability afterwards to explain why it didn't happen.
>
> —Winston Churchill, British politician

BELIEVE IT OR NOT

An occupational therapist completed a PhD program after twenty years working with a federal agency in the area of occupational therapy. Seeking a career change, he applied for a sociology position at a small college. During discussions with the dean, he agreed to create a new evening, part-time geriatric occupational therapy degree.

After joining the faculty as assistant professor, he built the program, creating courses, hiring part-time teachers, and recruiting students. The degree was an instant success.

In his first year, he noticed a distinct move to replace tenure-track faculty with instructors or adjuncts. He was assured this would not happen to him. Despite successes, he received occasional criticism from the dean and other professors.

QUESTION

What happened?

ANSWER

Halfway through year two of his contract, the dean called him into her office and charged him with making small offenses. Two weeks later, the department chair explained that his contract would not be renewed. He sent the following email to a friend.

> Hi Janet,
> You were right. Adjunct faculty will take over occupational therapy. My contract will not be renewed.
> I don't have to teach (this is my love) . . . just have to find my next teaching opportunity.
> On to the next adventure! Talk to you soon. Charles.

QUESTION

What was going on?

ANSWER

The incident reflects a person caught in the changing landscape of higher education. The tendency of institutions to move to contingent faculty is accompanied by a drive to build new degree programs. To establish them, the schools need a full-time commitment until courses are designed and instructors are identified. Then, the full-time professor is no longer critical. The shift from tenure-track to other appointments is a weak signal that affects all areas of the liberal arts.

WEAK SIGNALS

A weak signal is an early warning of change. It starts at low volume or is otherwise not obvious because it is lost in the noise of society. As the signal grows over time, it is often ignored or denied by people. Recent examples include global warming and unsustainable environment behaviors.

We cannot predict extreme events. Can we see weak signals and respond to them to achieve goals or avoid disasters?

PERCEPTUAL AND MENTAL SETS

In psychology, a set is a group of expectations that make us especially sensitive to specific kinds of information. It leads to a predisposition to perceive things in a certain way. Two kinds can be identified:

- **Perceptual Set.** We see or hear something that automatically triggers a response. People are distracted when they hear their name in a crowded room. When hungry, we instinctively recognize the faint aroma of food.
- **Mental Set.** We solve a problem or resolve a dilemma by force of habit from a belief formed at an earlier time. Someone starts a sentence and we finish it with a different meaning than is about to occur.

Perceptional and mental sets make it easy to reach a decision or solve a problem. At the same time, attachment to the wrong set inhibits decision making, problem solving, and creativity. It causes us to fail to make changes, no matter how desperately they are needed.

FINISHING SENTENCES

A psychological set is most noticeable when your thinking is moving faster than a situation unfolds. We tend to draw the wrong conclusions. The following unfinished sentences have no context to help understand what finishes them. Without weak signals, do you think you will guess the answers? They are given below.

Another word for jokes is __________.
It's a small world with __________.
Sleep is for people who __________.
Life must end and the way I want to go is __________.
Nobody likes a __________.
These scrambled eggs taste like __________.

QUESTION

A professor is successful using only a chalkboard and oral communication in the classroom. A school offers him training on audiovisual and internet tools. He rejects the possibilities. Why does he do that?

ANSWER

It could be the result of a predisposition. As a perceptual set, he may have had a bad experience with computers and refuses to use them. As a mental set, he may believe that step-by-step writing on a board allows time needed for student reflection and understanding.

HISTORICAL VIEW OF LIBERAL ARTS

Americans have a history of appreciating education and its impact on developing citizens and improving the quality of life. A four-year college degree was a path to financial success from almost any perspective from the end of World War II to today. Tables 6.1 through 6.5 contain weak signals on the importance of a college degree.

Table 6.1. Education Levels and Median Earnings (All ages full-time working)

Degree	*Percent of Population*	*Annual Earnings*
Less than high school diploma	7	27,000
High school diploma	26	37,000
Some college	16	42,000
Associate's degree	11	46,000
Bachelor's degree	25	61,000
Master's degree	11	75,000
Doctoral degree	2	100,000
Professional degree	2	111,000
Average		51,000

Table 6.2. Annual Earnings by Education Level and Age (2012 data)

Age	*High School Diploma*	*College, No Degree*	*Associate's Degree*	*Bachelor's Degree*
18	17,000	0	0	0
19	17,000	15,000	0	0
20	22,000	22,000	25,000	0
23	22,000	22,000	25,000	32,000
27	29,000	31,000	35,000	44,000
32	32,000	37,000	41,000	53,000
37	35,000	42,000	46,000	64,000
42	37,000	44,000	48,000	68,000
47	39,000	46,000	51,000	72,000
52	39,000	47,000	52,000	72,000
57	39,000	47,000	52,000	69,000
62	37,000	46,000	51,000	66,000

Table 6.3. Earnings Distribution (Percent; full-time year-round workers age thirty-five to forty-four, by education level, 2015)

Annual Earnings	*High School Diploma*	*College, No Degree*	*Associate's Degree*	*Bachelor's Degree*
Under $20,000	26	12	7	6
$20,000 to $39,999	50	41	36	30
$40,000 to $59,999	15	26	29	30
$60,000 to $79,999	6	11	15	19
$80,000 to $99,999	1	5	6	7
Over $100,000	2	5	7	8

Table 6.4. Median Earnings of Early Career and Mid-Career (College graduates working full time, by college major, 2013–2014)

Major	*Early Career*	*Mid-Career*
Computer science	$54,000	$86,000
Physics	$50,000	$80,000
Nursing	$48,000	$65,000
Economics	$48,000	$80,000
Finance	$47,000	$80,000
Accounting	$45,000	$68,000
Mathematics	$42,000	$77,000
General business	$40,000	$67,000
Chemistry	$39,000	$69,000
Political science	$38,000	$70,000
Business management	$38,000	$61,000
Communications	$36,000	$62,000
Philosophy	$35,000	$60,000
Journalism	$35,000	$64,000
History	$35,000	$60,000
Secondary education	$34,000	$47,700
Sociology	$33,000	$54,000
English language	$32,200	$55,000
Elementary education	$32,000	$42,000
Art history	$32,000	$53,000
Biology	$31,500	$60,000
Psychology	$30,000	$52,000
Early childhood education	$30,000	$40,000
Overall	$38,000	$62,000

Table 6.5. Unemployment Rates by Education Level (Percent; individuals age twenty-five and older, 1995 to 2015)

Year	High School Diploma	College, No Degree	Associate's Degree	Bachelor's Degree
1995	4.8	4.3	3.3	2.4
2000	3.4	2.9	2.3	1.7
2005	4.7	4.2	3.3	2.3
2010	10.3	9.2	7.0	4.7
2015	5.4	5.0	3.8	2.6

QUESTION

Most full-time college students work part-time and thus lose earnings compared to individuals who cease education after high school. On balance, was it a good financial decision to go to college from a recent historical perspective?

ANSWER

Yes, indeed. Compared to high school graduates, bachelor's degree holders overcome the cost of college and loss of earning by age thirty-five. Given the long life of earnings until age sixty-five or so, college was a good financial choice.

FUTURE VIEW OF LIBERAL ARTS

Many people are debating the future of higher education. A trichotomy has developed:

- **Liberal Arts, Business, and Education.** The traditional disciplines of Plato's Academy, augmented by business administration and education degrees with a required liberal arts foundation.
- **STEM.** The disciplines of science, technology, engineering, and mathematics. They stand on their own, are in high demand from students possessing the necessary math skills, and may or may not have a liberal arts foundation.
- **Vocational Areas.** The variety of programs that prepare students for specific careers, usually minus a liberal arts component.

ANSWERS ON FINISHING SENTENCES

How close were you?

- Another word for jokes is LIES.
- It's a small world with A BUNCH OF STUPID PEOPLE.
- Sleep is for people who DON'T SUBSCRIBE TO NETFLIX.
- Life must end and the way I want to go is TO BE ATTACKED BY CUTE PUPPIES.
- Nobody likes a TEENAGER.
- These scrambled eggs taste LIKE HEAVEN.

WEAK SIGNALS ON THE VALUE OF THE LIBERAL ARTS

Many advocates argue strongly that America needs people with STEM or vocational degrees. These areas have largely avoided the controversy on the value of college. It is much different for liberal arts, business, and education. These disciplines are challenged by emerging weak signals.

QUESTION

After adjusting for inflation, 2007 college graduates earned the same salaries as 1979 graduates. In the past ten years, starting salaries dropped 19 percent for male and 16 percent for female college graduates. Are these weak signals?

ANSWER

Could be.

QUESTION

A professor gave his class the questions and answers three days before an exam. When asked about the practice, he said it was the only way that many of the students could pass the course. Is this a weak signal?

ANSWER

Maybe. He explained, "My final exam is so comprehensive and detailed that students master the content by studying the exact questions." When pressed he also mentioned, "Well, many other teachers do the same thing. Our students don't buy the textbooks."

QUESTION

A professor claims she taught the same content in the same way for twenty years. When she started, she graded exams with a small percentage of As, Ds, and Fs, and mostly Bs and Cs. How is she doing today?

ANSWER

She curves the exams. Her rationale, "Half of my students would fail the course if I did not impose a strict formula to upgrade exam scores."

QUESTION

What is the significance of professors adjusting their courses as described in the previous questions?

ANSWER

Employers take these behaviors as weak signals that college graduates are not being prepared for the rigors of the workforce. This will affect future career opportunities for holders of bachelor's degrees.

TRUTHINESS: A WEAK SIGNAL FOR THE LIBERAL ARTS?

In 2016, college campuses were exposed to the degree that the presidential election in the United States revealed major flaws in how people view beliefs and facts. We had to confront new definitions of "truth." Not a big deal? It was to the editors of dictionaries.

"Truthiness" was Merriam-Webster's Word of the Year in 2006. It refers to a statement that can't be supported by logic or evidence. We know truthiness intuitively "from the gut" or because it "feels right." We completely ignore evidence, logic, intellectual examination, or contradictory information.

"Post-truth" was Oxford Dictionary's Word of the Year in 2016. It describes circumstances when appeals to emotion and personal belief shape public opinion despite sharply conflicting and largely accurate facts. Evidence is ignored as a message is accepted and repeated.

The concept of "truth" has been changing, but it exploded during the 2016 presidential campaign. Candidates vied for voter attention in a series of debates that captured the attention of a widely divided electorate: "The country is in serious trouble." "The economy is in great shape." "You are a crook." "She is a liar." "He is an idiot." Who should we believe?

We began to realize the extent to which people play with facts. Are they lying? The *Tampa Bay Times* sponsors a project, PolitiFact by name, that checks the "facts" in statements by politicians, lobbyists, and interest groups. It proclaims itself to be a non-partisan effort.

In the 2016 election campaign, PolitiFact graded the statements of Democratic and Republican candidates. It found dozens of questionable statements identified as "mostly true," "half true," "mostly false," "false," and "pants on fire." How can we like a serious intellectual effort where a category of truth can be "pants on fire"?

The sad truth about 2016 politics was that a person was able to get elected by appealing to sticky messages that have no substance. Truth is nowhere to be found because we ignore messages that conflict with what we believe. Don't blame the media. The fault is ours. We believe what sounds good. But does it make sense?

- "A diamond is forever." Does it really matter when a woman's lifespan is eighty or so years?
- "Maxwell House: Good to the last drop." Who drinks coffee to the last drop?
- "BMW: The Ultimate Driving Machine." Better than Ferrari?

Advertising slogans are one thing. It is far more dangerous for students to be guided by false statements that do not address the risks they face after graduation. Does it hurt them when they cannot or do not separate truth from falsehood? When they try to manage the risks in our lives, shouldn't they know the difference?

Does anybody really care about the truth? Of course they do. Pick a version. This is not a good situation.

CONCLUSION AND FALLACIES

Historical data shows incredible value to having a college degree. People interpret the data in terms of their perceptual and mental sets and may or may not tune themselves to weak signals that change is occurring. When we hold strong beliefs in something, like for example the value of a liberal arts education, it is easy to ignore or rationalize weak signals that provide contrary information. Sometimes we need to put aside our assumptions and consider other possibilities. Hence:

Fallacy 6. Attacks on higher education result from a misunderstanding of what we do.

Reality 6. Weak signals encourage us to respond to legitimate concerns about what we do.

Chapter Seven

Are Liberals and Conservatives at War on the Campus? Could Professors Have a Bias?

The reason I talk to myself is because I'm the only one whose answers I accept.

—George Carlin, American comedian

POLITICAL AND SOCIAL PHILOSOPHY OF PROFESSORS

To some degree, people easily fall into two camps in terms of their beliefs. It will surprise no one that professors do, too:

- **Liberals.** They believe the government should alleviate social ills, protect individual and human rights, and ensure no one is in need.
- **Conservatives.** They believe we should retain traditional social institutions in the framework of our culture and civilization.

QUESTION

The seas are rough and the ship is sinking. The only lifeboat holds a maximum of six people. Ten people are on board. The four individuals who do not leave with the lifeboat will surely die. Who would you save?

1. You, the captain of the ship
2. Bill Gates
3. Special education high school teacher

4. Woman who is six weeks pregnant
5. Husband of the pregnant woman
6. Thirty-two-year-old hospital emergency room nurse
7. Pope Francis
8. Ten-year-old twin boy
9. Twin sister of the ten-year-old boy
10. Twenty-two-year-old marine veteran of Iraq war

ANSWER

People give different answers based on beliefs. We already discussed this.

QUESTION

The economy is rough and the college is downsizing. Only six people can survive. Who would you save?

1. You, the dean of the college
2. Full-time grief counselor
3. Full professor in theology
4. Associate professor in economics
5. Assistant professor in psychology
6. Director of academic computing
7. Information systems support manager
8. Coach of the winning football team
9. Your own excellent administrative assistant
10. Director of the honors program

QUESTION

Who would be saved if we ask college instructors, one each part-time, full-time temporary, tenure-track, and tenured?

ANSWER

Whatever your answer, a regional difference would be noted. Let's look at that.

BIAS IN THE PROFESSORIATE

Colin Woodard is the author of two seminal works on cultural bias in North America. He identifies eleven regions. For higher education, we can modify them into five categories. Somewhat broadly, we find:

- **New York and New England.** Professors seek to create a perfect society, welcome immigrants, and promote educational achievement. The role of government is to control greedy politicians and corporations.
- **New York City and Surrounding Area.** Professors encourage a multiethnic, multireligious, and highly materialistic culture demanding individual rights and freedom to speak.
- **Deep South.** Professors are part of a stronghold of white supremacy, aristocratic order, and privilege for the few. They resist environmental improvement, labor reform, consumer safety protection, and taxation of the wealthy.
- **Middle America.** Professors reject ethnic purity, oppressive ideology or regulation, and intrusions in daily life. They historically reflect the values of the American middle class.
- **The Pacific Coast.** Professors lead movements marked by idealism, social reform, and self-exploration.

QUESTION

Of liberals and conservatives, which has people who are averse to change?

ANSWER

Everybody is averse to change if things are going their way.

QUESTION

Of liberals and conservatives, which has people who want things to change today?

ANSWER

Everybody wants changes for the things that are not going their way.

QUESTION

The freedom of inquiry associated with the academy produces a philosophy: "I disapprove of what you say, but I will defend to the death your right to say it." Is this a liberal or conservative viewpoint?

ANSWER

If the rhetoric on campus accompanying the 2017 presidential race is any indication, the saying has been updated to, "I disapprove of what you say, so shut up and leave the campus."

CONSERVATIVE AND LIBERAL POLITICAL HUMOR

Social media allows individuals to post any messages they want within certain legal and criminal boundaries. Some postings by both conservatives and liberals are attempts at humor. Examples:

- Did you hear about the new presidential diet? You let Putin eat your lunch every day.
- How does the president win the war on terror? He renames it the overseas contingency operation.
- They say the president is just like Christopher Columbus. When he left to discover America, Columbus didn't know where he was going and when he got there he didn't know where he was.
- What do you get when you offer the president a penny for his thoughts? Change.
- What's the difference between the president and government bonds? Government bonds will mature someday.

QUESTION

Many people identify Republicans with conservative humor and Democrats with liberal humor. Of these attempts at humor, how can we tell conservatives and liberals apart?

ANSWER

Ask the person using the humor the name of the president. If it's Clinton or Obama, it is Republican humor. Bush or Trump are associated with Democratic humor.

QUESTION

How can the same joke apply to both parties?

ANSWER

A person schooled in the liberal arts should be able to answer that question.

LIBERAL BIAS IN THE ACADEMY

If we follow the trail of the liberal arts all to way to creating an educated person, we find liberal and conservative wisdom and folly. This creates an interesting quandary. More than 75 percent of professors seem to fit the description of liberals.

Nicholas Kristof wrote a 2016 article in the *New York Times* pointing out evidence of liberal domination of the professoriate in American colleges and universities. He argues that:

- Ninety or so percent of faculty members are Democrats or Independents.
- Marxists are prominent in social science disciplines.
- Academics support the rights of women, blacks, Latinx, gays, and Muslims unless they espouse conservative agendas.
- Academics dismiss the beliefs of conservatives as lacking intellectual honesty and diversity.
- Academia discriminates against Republicans and evangelicals.
- Academics do not discriminate against others but accept them only if they agree with a liberal viewpoint.

CONCLUSION AND FALLACIES

We have considerable evidence that liberal and conservative professors have contentious interaction on college campuses. They look at the same set of "facts" and draw different points of emphasis based on their beliefs. Hence:

Fallacy 7. Professors study the evidence and present a balanced perspective to their students.
Reality 7. Professors by and large are biased along liberal or conservative lines.

Chapter Eight

Do Reputation and Accreditation Matter? Would Anyone Hire Plato if He Did Not Have a Doctoral Degree?

If you want to be respected by others, the great thing is to respect yourself. Only by that . . . will you compel others to respect you.

—Fyodor Dostoyevsky, Russian author

BELIEVE IT OR NOT

Three economics professors decided to offer consulting services. They included the name Princeton in their company title. One client wanted to meet Swiss bankers so a professor using the Princeton consulting title requested and got an appointment.

As the professor and client ended the visit in Zurich, a Swiss banker said, "So, are you a professor at the university?" As no university was specified and seeing no need to extend the departure, the professor answered, "Well, yes."

Some people may disagree with the answer, as the individual was not a professor at Princeton University. Absent this misconception, the Swiss bank may have denied the request to visit.

Academic reputation makes a difference. Reality is more problematic. Students, parents, and would-be professors often equate success with a tenured position at a top-ranked school. Do these environments work for undergraduates pursuing the benefits of the liberal arts? Let's take a look.

CHARACTERISTICS OF LIBERAL ARTS COLLEGES

Most liberal arts colleges follow the same pattern of instruction:

- A broad array of traditional liberal arts subjects during the first half of the college experience
- Residential instruction for full-time students
- Small class size with heavy reliance on student participation
- Student-teacher mentoring, interaction, and collaboration with professors in contrast to lectures by research-oriented professors and discussions with graduate teaching assistants

CHARACTERISTICS OF "LIBERAL ARTS" DEGREES

Discussions about a liberal arts education often fail to understand liberal arts colleges. The traditional four-year program has two parts:

- **Lower Division.** Breadth in the liberal arts.
- **Upper Division.** Focus in a narrower area, commonly business, education, or a liberal art.

Once students have the foundation, they can apply their knowledge in professional areas. Thus, an expansion of a concept:

> A student who completes a liberal arts foundation has a liberal arts degree even when the major field is in education, business, pre-law, or other professional discipline.

LIBERAL ARTS COLLEGES GEOGRAPHICALLY

North America has more than eighteen hundred four-year colleges and universities, with 90 percent offering a liberal arts foundation. Hundreds identify themselves as "liberal arts" institutions. Some geographical examples in 2016:

State	*Number*
New York	51
Pennsylvania	46
Massachusetts	28
Illinois	26
California	23
Canada	22
Texas	18
Georgia	17
Vermont	12

The number of liberal arts institutions drops precipitously outside the United States. More than half of European countries do not have even a single designated liberal arts college. Only five countries have more than one. India has the most in Asia, followed by Pakistan and Japan. Africa has only one. The numbers:

Country	*Number*
Netherlands	8
United Kingdom	3
Germany	3
France	2
Sweden	2
India	11
Pakistan	5
Japan	4
Australia	4
Africa (Ghana)	1

LIBERAL ARTS EDUCATION WITHIN BIG UNIVERSITIES

Most large universities offer a foundation of liberal arts in professional degree programs. Here we have a problem. The classes often meet in large lecture halls with limited student participation and student-teacher mentoring and interaction. We will deal with this situation throughout the book by addressing reforms to modernize the liberal arts experience.

ACADEMIC RANKING OF INSTITUTIONS

Multiple organizations publish annual rankings of the world's best colleges and universities. Three most influential and widely recognized are:

- **Academic Ranking of World Universities.** An effort began by Shanghai Jiaotong University in 2003.
- **QS World University Rankings.** Published by a British company to help students evaluate learning opportunities around the world.
- **THE World University Rankings.** Published by a British magazine specializing in higher education.

TOP TWENTY-FIVE UNIVERSITIES IN THE WORLD

The three authorities agree the top schools are largely located in the United States and United Kingdom. This can be seen from summary data of the top twenty-five schools. Twenty-one U.S. and six U.K. schools make at least one of the three lists. The Academic Ranking of World Universities is skewed most heavily to U.S. schools.

COUNTRY DISTRIBUTION OF RANKINGS

The United States and United Kingdom have the most top-ranked institutions:

	Academic Ranking of World Universities	*QS World University Rankings*	*THE World University Rankings*	*All*
Canada	1	1		2
China		2	1	1
Japan	1	1		2
Singapore			2	2
Switzerland	1	2	2	2
United Kingdom	4	5	6	6
United States	18	14	13	21
Total	25	25	25	36

All three lists agree on seventeen schools in the top twenty-five. Based on an average ranking, Harvard is number one followed by Stanford and the Massachusetts Institute of Technology. Cambridge and Oxford are four and five. ETH Zurich is the only non-U.S. or -U.K. school to make all three lists.

SCHOOLS ON ALL THREE LISTS

Seventeen schools make all three lists:

	Rank	Academic Ranking of World Universities	QS World University Rankings	THE World University Rankings
1. Harvard	1.37	1	1	3
2. Stanford	2.33	2	3	2
3. Massachusetts Institute of Technology	2.67	5	2	1
4. Cambridge	4.00	4	4	4
5. Oxford	6.00	7	5	6
6. California Institute of Technology	7.67	8	10	5
7. Princeton	8.00	6	7	11
8. Chicago	10.33	10	11	10
9. Yale	11.33	11	8	15
10. Columbia	12.67	9	9	20
11. University College London	14.67	17	20	7
12. Cornell	15.33	13	17	16
13. ETH Zurich	15.33	19	19	8
14. Imperial College London	15.33	22	15	9
15. Pennsylvania	17.33	18	16	18
16. Johns Hopkins	18.33	16	22	17
17. Michigan	20.00	23	14	23

Other schools to make at least one list were University of California, Berkeley; University of California, San Diego; University of California, San Francisco; Duke; EPFL Lausanne; King's College London; London School of Econ; Nanyang Tech (Singapore); National Singapore; Peking; The Australian National; The Edinburgh; Tokyo; Toronto; New York University; University of California, Los Angeles; Tsinghua; Washington in St. Louis; and the University of Washington.

QUESTION

Six of the eight Ivy League schools make the top seventeen. Does the failure by two schools to make the list harm the superstar status of the Ivy League?

ANSWER

Probably not. Brown University is number fifty-one and Dartmouth is eighty-two.

PROFESSOR MAAS, POPULAR TEACHER

Psychology 101 at Cornell University enrolls as many as sixteen hundred students in a single lecture hall with bare floors and hard-backed wooden seats. Professor James Maas has taught the course for more than thirty years. It is one of the most popular classes on campus.

QUESTION

Professor Maas may do his students a disservice. In such a large hall, can students in the back read what he writes on the blackboard?

ANSWER

No. He never writes anything. Minimal lecturing is mixed with constant exercises, games, and large-screen slides and videos.

QUESTION

Is his failure to interact with the students a disservice?

ANSWER

Not at all. He does interact. An example is when he gives them a list of unrelated words such as monkey-tomato, kidney-automobile, citizen-eyeball, and factory-kangaroo. He divides the class into two groups of students. One is asked to memorize the terms using the words themselves. The other is asked to memorize pictures of the words. When tested in a few minutes, the group using pictures remembered more terms. The lesson is that imagery can be a powerful memory aid.

QUESTION

Does such a lesson have any value in the real world?

ANSWER

Yeah. Start with an understanding of how visual impact applies in advertising, fashions, communications, and beyond.

QUESTION

He makes only three or four points in each lecture, but students in his class are tested with multiple choice exams. Where do they get the details they need to answer questions?

ANSWER

The course has the usual textbook and computer programs to be used outside the classroom. The university provides teaching assistants available twelve hours a day to help students as needed.

QUESTION

How important is the student popularity of Professor Maas to Cornell's reputation?

ANSWER

Not a lot really. He has won teaching awards but is best known for his work in the field of sleep research.

REGIONAL VERSUS PROFESSIONAL ACCREDITATION

Accreditation is defined as a certification of competence in a specified subject area by an outside body recognized in that area. It applies to a program or school and conveys professional approval.

Institutional accreditation has benefits. Students can transfer their credits to other accredited institutions. The government and banks will lend them money to pay tuition. Employers may give preference to graduates of accredited institutions.

In the United States, colleges and universities can achieve two levels of accreditation:

- **Regional Accreditation.** Accrediting agencies are private educational associations recognized by the government. They develop criteria and conduct evaluations to determine if a college meets required standards.
- **Professional Accreditation.** This is a recognition by a professional society or other organization of specific programs including education, business, engineering, and nursing.

Accreditation is an evaluation by the school's peers and thus is called a peer-review process.

QUESTION

Some people argue regional and professional accreditation are virtually the same. Is this true?

ANSWER

No. Regional accreditation is like licensing a business in a jurisdiction. It conveys a status that qualifies a school for student financial aid and other federal and state assistance. Some professional accreditations are optional. They claim to achieve a high standard of providing knowledge in a specific area.

QUESTION

What is the primary benefit for a U.S. college to obtain accreditation in the view of an optimist?

ANSWER

It shows parents and students that a school is meeting high standards.

QUESTION

What is the primary benefit to obtain accreditation in the view of a pessimist?

ANSWER

It qualifies its students to apply for financial aid from the federal government.

QUESTION

What is the primary benefit to obtain accreditation as seen by a college struggling to meet the paperwork requirements prior to a visit by an accreditation team?

ANSWER

It has no benefits at all and simply means a school must do a lot of unnecessary documentation of what it already does well.

QUESTION

Some educators believe an "accredited status" means students and the public can expect a school to fulfill its promises. This applies to delivering a solid liberal arts education. Are they right?

ANSWER

Maybe not. The U.S. Department of Education revoked the federal recognition of Acics, an accrediting body, in 2016 after two of its accredited schools closed unexpectedly, stranding thousands of students prior to graduation.

QUESTION

Other educators believe a degree from an accredited school has more value than one from a non-accredited school. Are they right?

ANSWER

Sometimes.

QUESTION

Accreditation involves preparation of a self-prepared report on school activities, a visit by a team to the campus, and a team recommendation to the accrediting agency. This process supports sharing best practices. Is this true?

ANSWER

Probably.

QUESTION

Some professors believe that any four-year, degree-granting college or university that follows traditional accreditation guidelines can be the home base for academic success. Are they right?

ANSWER

Maybe. It depends upon expectations. As soon as a professor achieves any status, most efforts for recognition tend to be tied to the ranking of the institution.

QUESTION

A school applied for a professional accreditation that required 75 percent PhD coverage in teaching and an average research output equal to one journal per full-time faculty member per year. The school had twenty-three faculty members but only six total publications each year. It hired three new professors who had eighteen journal articles a year among them. Did the school successfully achieve accreditation?

ANSWER

No. The visitation team concluded that the guideline was misunderstood. Recognition for an institution does not come from a few overachievers. Rather, achievement should be distributed across the faculty.

QUESTION

To increase the chance for professional accreditation, a dean hired six faculty members with publications but inadequate English-language skills to effectively teach undergraduates. Does this meet the scholarship requirements for most accreditation teams?

ANSWER

Nope. Although scholarship is often the primary factor in successful efforts to achieve professional accreditation, most associations consider the full picture. Too many teachers who are not capable in the classroom can be a decisive factor in a negative decision.

Enough on accreditation. Now we move on to the public and private view of the status of a school.

QUESTION

An accrediting body recommends testing in eight areas in a single written exam taken in the final semester before a student graduates. The school requires full-time students to cover each area in a specific course over a four-year period. Then, using modern technology, the exam is taken online from any computer. The results do not affect course grades or count toward graduation.

When students open the link on the website and start the two hundred questions on the multiple choice exam, they can stop and return multiple times but must finish within seventy-two hours. Does this provide useful information on learning that occurred?

ANSWER

Not likely. Lots of problems.

- **Time Lag Since Study.** Students will remember fewer details for courses taken earlier in the program. The exam only tests long-term memory, not initial learning.
- **Consistency of Results.** Some students will not make much effort. Why try hard to "pass" the exam if it does not count toward a degree?

QUESTION

On a professional accrediting exam, one student got 28 percent right and finished in forty-five minutes. Another got 92 percent taking more than six hours to finish. Does this show the need to encourage students to be more dedicated when taking the exam?

ANSWER

Not really. Without controls, the results reflect self-monitoring by students who can receive markedly different scores aside from their knowledge. A follow up showed the first student guessed randomly while the second student looked up answers on the Internet.

HARVARD'S REPUTATION

We can have every conceivable discussion about reputation and still not alter one permanent fact. Harvard is number one. Is it the great professors, the bright students, or the massive endowment? Let's look at how the school's reputation makes things work for its graduates.

QUESTION

Did any U.S. president receive his undergraduate education at Harvard University?

ANSWER

Yes. John Adams, John Quincy Adams, Rutherford B. Hayes, Theodore Roosevelt, Franklin D. Roosevelt, and John F. Kennedy.

QUESTION

How did President Kennedy prepare for the admission process to Harvard?

ANSWER

He was born. With his powerful father behind him, he barely applied. After attaining mediocre high school grades, he wrote a five-sentence essay to explain why he wanted to go to Harvard. The only clarity was the thought, "To be a 'Harvard man' is an enviable distinction, and one that I sincerely hope I shall attain."

Harvard, like other of America's premier universities, has long been the sanctuary of the elite. Harvard's students come largely from a background of economic privilege. Their median family income is $168,800. Three percent are from the top one-tenth of 1 percent. The breakdown:

Percent of Students	
From top 0.1%	3%
From top 1%	15%
From top 5%	39%
From top 10%	53%
From top 20%	67%
From bottom 20%	4.5%

QUESTION

How do Harvard students do economically later in life?

ANSWER

Not bad at all. The median individual income at age thirty-four is $82,000, with men at $96,000 and women at $70,000. The breakdown:

Percent of Alumni	
In the top 1 percent	21 percent
In the top 5 percent	42 percent
In the top 10 percent	52 percent
In the top 20 percent	65 percent
In the bottom 20 percent	9 percent

ARE ELITE SCHOOLS DIFFERENT?

Is the picture of Harvard students an isolated snapshot? Not at all. Harvard ranks only seventh of the list of richest family incomes among the top twelve elite institutions. Brown has the highest.

Average Family Income		
1	Brown	$204,200
2	Dartmouth	$200,400
3	Penn	$195,500
4	Yale	$192,600
5	Duke	$186,700
6	Princeton	$186,100
7	Harvard	$168,800
8	Stanford	$167,500
9	Cornell	$151,600
10	Columbia	$150,900
11	Massachusetts Institute of Technology	$137,400
12	University of Chicago	$134,500

QUESTION

What about a student from a poor family who goes to Harvard? Can a poor student become a rich adult?

ANSWER

Definitely yes. At Harvard, 58 percent of the students who were from the bottom fifth of income as students moved to the top fifth as adults. Once again, Harvard was not on top of the list of elite colleges: alumni from top schools earn more money after graduation. One statistic tracks the percent of alumni who grew up in a family in the lowest fifth of incomes and eventually reached the top fifth themselves. The schools that have the most upward movement are:

1	Massachusetts Institute of Technology	67%
2	Princeton	66%
3	Stanford	63%
4	Columbia	61%
5	Cornell	59%
6	Penn	58%
7	Harvard	58%
8	Yale	57%
9	Brown	53%
10	Duke	50%
11	Dartmouth	50%
12	University of Chicago	45%

QUESTION

Does reputation matter?

ANSWER

Maybe. This book could be titled, *Memoirs of a Wanna-be Harvard Professor Currently Teaching at Saint Peter's University*. What makes us Harvard professors? If the truth be told, it is the hope of many of the 1.7 million instructors in higher education today. We may start at Towson State College, but Harvard may send us an invitation once our dissertation is published. We are still waiting.

CONCLUSION AND FALLACIES

A school's reputation is based upon many factors. A link between school status and successful liberal arts preparation is not obvious. Some well-known universities do not seem to care much at all about undergraduate education. Family wealth may correlate more to success than the education. The role of accrediting bodies is also not clear. Hence:

Fallacy 8. Reputation and accreditation are the earmarks of a successful liberal arts education.

Reality 8. Reputation and accreditation can be quite misleading in the search for the liberal arts.

Part III

REVISING THE PROFESSORIATE

Chapter Nine

Do We Still Need Professors in the Classroom? Why Are We Paying These People?

It is much more difficult to measure nonperformance than performance.

—Harold S. Geneen, American businessman

FACULTY VALUE AND COMPENSATION

Critics of faculty reward systems argue that colleges value research more than teaching. A 2017 paper from The National Bureau of Economic Research supports that contention, with evidence that the highest-paid faculty members teach fewer undergraduates than their lower-paid colleagues. The paper also suggests that valuing research output over teaching doesn't necessarily affect educational quality.

QUESTION

What is missing from the National Bureau of Economic Research study?

ANSWER

It fails to capture the real essence of faculty compensation. Is there really any relationship between faculty value and compensation or other rewards in the academy? Why do schools pay professors?

THE GREAT SHAME OF OUR PROFESSION

Earlier we met Kevin Birmingham.When he accepted the Truman Capote Award in 2017, his speech touched on faculty compensation. It offers a reflective view of contradictions of academic rewards.

He started by addressing an injustice from his belief that he is the first adjunct faculty member to receive the award. He points out he is "one of over one million . . . instructors working on a temporary or contingent basis" not knowing if they will be teaching in the next term or if their classes will be cancelled with a few days' notice. He quotes statistics:

- Tenured faculty represent 17 percent of college instructors.
- Part-time adjuncts are the majority of the professoriate and its fastest-growing segment.
- The part-time designation is misleading as nine out of ten adjuncts work at more than one institution. The average instructor has annual earnings of about $17,000.
- The median compensation is less than $3,000 a course. The maximum at top schools is about $6,000.
- Twenty-five percent of contingent faculty receive public assistance including Medicaid or food stamps.

Birmingham started his speech on compensation even though his invitation was to address literary criticism. His rationale? The professoriate has become fearful, insular, and conformist. Junior faculty restrict their behavior conceptually, politically, and formally. Professors are not paid to perform. For many, they are lucky to be paid at all. His book exists only because he was willing to give up a tenure-track job to write it.

QUESTION

What is the takeaway from Kevin Birmingham?

ANSWER

He is arguing for a return to the old days. The great shame is blamed on the academy. This may be misplaced. If the world has changed, pay for performance is changing also. For most professors, unfettered scholarship is not enough. Why do we pay professors? Let's question the question.

PAYING PEOPLE TO TEACH

A professor starts a class asking students, "Do any of you get paid by a company or other organization?" As mature working adults taking evening classes, they seem puzzled by the question. "Yes, of course." A follow-up question is, "Why does someone pay you?" No problem with that one. "We work . . . get results . . . perform tasks . . . get things done . . . pursue goals." The list goes on and on.

When the professor asks if they think he gets paid, they say yes. The school pays him to help them learn. He denies that allegation. It is not necessary for them to learn anything. He gets paid if he meets ten classes in the academic term. He simply must be in the room to get paid. At this point, he asks some questions.

QUESTION

"We are scheduled to meet this class for three and half hours. Suppose I let you go early. Does the school dock my pay?"

ANSWER

Everyone agrees the answer is no.

QUESTION

"Suppose I die at the halfway point in the class. Does the school have to pay the full stipend?"

ANSWER

Students think the answer is yes.

QUESTION

"What if a teacher dies halfway through a class and no one notices?"

ANSWER

Students find this question to be amusing or perhaps silly.

PAYING PEOPLE TO MAKE LAMPS

Then it gets serious. “Assume we have two workers who can produce lamps perfectly to specifications with no defects. The first individual produces eight lamps an hour. The second worker finishes ten an hour. Which is the better worker?”

ANSWER

Most people instinctively identify the second worker as superior. When asked why, they think the answer is obvious. The company is paying less for fabrication of each lamp.

QUESTION

Our final question is, “What is the underlying assumption of your answer that ten lamps are better than eight?”

ANSWER

Most students do not realize that ten is better than eight only if we pay people for time. If we pay people for per unit of the product, we do not care how long it takes to make it.

PROFESSORIAL SKILLS

We cannot discuss performance in higher education without tying it to the components of skills. If all other considerations are equal, which of the following is the best candidate for a professorial opening?

- **One hundred percent qualified**. The person has many years of experience and has done the job. A full professor with tenure.

- **Seventy-five percent qualified**. An associate professor with tenure.
- **Fifty percent qualified**. An assistant professor with five years teaching experience.
- **Twenty-five percent qualified**. A newly minted PhD with limited teaching experience.

The answer involves many considerations. Will a highly qualified person be motivated to prove anything? Do we want a combination of experience and room for growth? Should we take someone with no teaching experience?

QUESTION

Colleges overwhelmingly prefer to hire newly minted PhDs. What does this tell us?

ANSWER

They don't care about performance and don't want to pay for it.

QUESTION

The next question adds attitude to skills. We assume good attitude and good skills would be the first preference when hiring. If that person is not available, is the second preference a good attitude and poor skills or a poor attitude and good skills?

ANSWER

Responses indicate:

- **Good Attitude, Poor Skills.** This is the most common choice outside the academy. Employers are willing to mentor new employees, provide job relevant training, and modify duties.
- **Poor Attitude, Good Skills.** This is often overlooked when hiring assistant professors. Completion of a dissertation overcomes other evidence that an applicant is a poor match for the needs of the department or institution.

QUESTION

This question deals with balancing attitude and skills. Two professorial candidates are under consideration. One has a good attitude with limited teaching experience. The other has a poor attitude with excellent scholarship. Who will be preferred?

ANSWER

In the academy, we routinely value scholarship, or at least the PhD degree from a well-known university, and ignore evidence that an applicant is kind of grumpy.

COMPENSATION FOR PERFORMANCE

Now we make a major detour to the philosophy on the compensation of individuals. At the same time, money is always a factor and emotions are part of the equation.

QUESTION

Which of the following most closely describes your view of how a university should pay an applicant for a faculty position?

- Below market
- At market
- Above market
- Well above market

ANSWER

Within colleges and universities, most people respond that schools should match the market. Outside academia, the most common response is to pay above market.

QUESTION

What do people say when we ask, "How do you want to be paid yourself?"

ANSWER

This question can produce confusion. Outside academia, everyone seems to know they really want to be paid well above market. Above market at the least. With professors, the question comes out of nowhere. For whatever reason, they don't identify with it.

MEASURING PERFORMANCE

At this point let's tell the story of a computer software development project where six hundred programmers worked together for more than a year. The company had two job categories. A systems analyst had a great deal of prior experience. A programmer was less experienced and qualified. The company paid systems analysts twice as much money as programmers. It compared the average productivity of each group.

People were asked to estimate productivity. They knew the break-even point in compensation is analysts should be twice as productive as programmers. Who was worth more? Most people thought the company lost money on decisions to hire more analysts.

QUESTION

How much more efficient were systems analysts at completing tasks?

ANSWER

At twice the average salary, the analysts produced **five times as much usable code**. This is a story from IBM when it was developing the 360 computer. These results were reported in a 1975 book titled *The Mythical Man-Month: Essays on Software Engineering.* Since its publication, executives at top companies have looked for the best performers and paid them handsomely.

QUESTION

How does the IBM story apply to hiring professors for the Academy?

ANSWER

Most of the time it does not. Professors are not compensated for performance. They are often ill-equipped to discuss it. The school does not care the level or quality of the publications of individual professors. Mediocrity in the classroom is tolerated or blamed on the students.

PROFESSOR PERFORMANCE

Organizations use performance appraisals to identify strengths and weaknesses and determine who should be paid more, promoted, demoted, or fired. They are a staple of hierarchical organizations. In colleges and universities, they are largely a waste of time. Some problems:

- **Stressful.** Deans and chairs find it painful to deal with shortcomings and dread the process. Professors tend to overreact to negative comments.
- **Tension Afterwards.** The days, weeks, and months after an appraisal can be a period of tension.
- **Uneven Comparisons.** Some deans are excellent at completing appraisal forms. Others not so much.
- **Evaluator Bias.** Deans like some people and dislike others.
- **Differing Styles.** Appraisals are affected by differences in lecturing, use of the textbook, and methods of interacting with students.

QUESTION

A department chair conducted the evaluation of a professor three weeks prior to the end of a semester. One of the criticisms was student complaints about not learning much in the classroom. What did the professor do?

ANSWER

True story. The professor met his classes and assigned an added term paper saying something like, “You are complaining about not learning enough. This assignment will fix that problem.”

QUESTION

Did the assignment of the term paper cause problems for the department chair and dean?

ANSWER

Take a guess.

THE AVERAGE PROFESSOR

Another problem is that few professors think they are average. They are not alone. A survey of chief executive officers once asked, "How do you rank among your peers?" Ninety percent of the chief executive officers responded that they ranked in the top 10 percent of chief executive officers. Professors seem to have the same feeling.

QUESTION

What is the worst thing a dean can say about a professor on a performance appraisal?

ANSWER

The worst thing is to call the professor "average." According to the faculty guide, "Tenure is reserved for the exceptional." Everybody knows that is nonsense.

PERFORMANCE BIAS

Still one more problem of faculty appraisal systems is hidden bias. It can be conscious or subconscious. We can hate a person's scholarship, participation in faculty meetings, or personal hygiene.

QUESTION

A tenured professor agreed to serve on a promotion and tenure committee after refusing to serve on any committee for the previous eight years. Why?

ANSWER

When asked he explained that a good friend was coming up for promotion to full professor and he wanted to be sure he got it.

FORMAL APPRAISALS

Detailed performance appraisals in academia are not even needed for legal reasons. Most appointments give colleges a wide leeway to hire and fire. Absent obvious discrimination, only fixed contracts and tenure protect against arbitrary dismissal.

A meaningful evaluation might be simply a mentoring process with some evidence from observation and student feedback. Institutions might ask:

- Did he or she do the job?
- Did he or she engage his or her colleagues and students?
- Do we like him or her?

QUESTION

Is the recommendation to end formal faculty evaluations likely to be accepted?

ANSWER

Of course not. We can dream. In the meantime, maybe we can reform the things we can fix.

CONCLUSION AND FALLACIES

Colleges and universities rarely reward professors for their scholarship or performance in the classroom. Reform is needed. Some professors can be valued as scholars and others as teachers. The current hiring and evaluation processes are faulty at best and unfortunate at worst. Hence:

Fallacy 9. Colleges and universities pay professors to undertake research, develop student skills, and engage scholars and students.

Reality 9. Scholarship and engaging students often has no link to compensation or other rewards in the academy.

Chapter Ten

Does the Classroom Offer Status for Professors? When Was the Last Time Anyone Praised Your Teaching?

I don't like being famous—it is like a prison. And driving for Ferrari would make it far worse.

—Valentino Rossi, Italian professional motorcycle racer

BELIEVE IT OR NOT

Benito Mussolini was a teacher, politician, and journalist who rose to the position of prime minister and brought Italy into World War II. As a leader of the Italian Socialist movement, he founded the Fascist Party.

Early in his regime, Italians noticed an improvement in rail service. It occurred because of plans and actions taken before Mussolini took office. The fascist propaganda took credit promoting a slogan that Mussolini "made the trains run on time." It was an overstatement but people around the world bought it.

THE MUSSOLINI DECEPTION

We have a similar situation in the academy with the reputation of professors. For shorthand, let's call it the Mussolini Deception. It occurs when professors claim credit for creating important research that barely moves the indicator of human knowledge. Clusters of professors get together, cite each other's works, and accept each other's research into journals they themselves edit.

Many people accept the fallacious argument that only peer-reviewed academic journals are worthy of respect. Only when we take a closer look do we realize much of the research is obscure and findings are trivial. The claim for significance is as bogus as the claim that Mussolini made the trains run on time.

PROFESSOR ALAN SOKAL PRANK

In 1996, Duke University Press published a paper by Professor Alan Sokal. The title was, "Transgressing the Boundaries: Towards a Transformative Hermeneutics of Quantum Gravity." Sokal subsequently announced that his paper was an effort to reform academic scholarship. He called it outright nonsense describing it as "left-wing cant, fawning references, grandiose quotations, and outright nonsense."

Can a professor develop a meaningful reputation by writing for peer-reviewed journals? Let's check it out.

THE PURSUIT OF SUPERSTAR PROFESSORS

Websites regularly identify highly paid professors and point to a fierce competition as universities seek to attract superstar professors. One list recently identified the top ten highest-paid professors:

- Two medical doctors at Columbia and Cornell with $4 million and $3 million dollar salaries.
- One finance professor at Yale at $2.5 million.
- Two business professors at Harvard and Duke making $1 million dollars.
- Three professors at Thunderbird and one each at Texas, Austin and University of California, Berkeley, making $500,000 to $700,000.

When this information was published, the average salary for all U.S. professors with ten or more years of experience was $89,000.

DEPAUL HIRES A SUPERSTAR

Now we expose a simple truth. Superstar professors are not being paid to teach students or even to encourage learning. Michael Eric Dyson illustrated this point in 1999 when he took a position at DePaul University in Chicago.

The school hired him to link DePaul to issues of culture, race, and social justice. After finishing his doctorate at Princeton, he made a name for himself as a nationally known author, "hip-hop" scholar, articulate speaker, and even Baptist minister. A prolific writer, his viewpoints were eagerly sought by politicians, educators, and others.

A senior administrator at DePaul pointed out,

> We . . . are attracted by the fact that he is a public intellectual who has . . . linked the humanities and traditional areas of the university with . . . issues facing our larger society. (Richard J. Meister, "DePaul Hires High-Profile Culture Scholar," *Chicago Tribute*, April 29, 1999)

DePaul gave him a "university-wide professorship." At a school where the typical professor taught six to eight courses a year, Dyson taught two. DePaul proudly proclaimed it had a superstar professor but the relationship did not last long. In 2007, Dyson was lured away to Georgetown University.

QUESTION

In 2016, the University of Texas expanded its STARs program, adding $60 million to a fund for recruiting "superstar" faculty and "rising stars." Three nationally respected researchers in Asian history, French literature, and psychology applied as did two newly minted PhDs in biology and American studies. Do these individuals qualify for the increased funding offered through the STARs programs?

ANSWER

Nope. STARs stands for Science and Technology Acquisition and Retention. Forget the liberal arts types.

PROFESSOR AS SUPERSTAR

Professors elicit a high level of awe. They just have a look, an attitude. We cannot deny it. This is no longer high school where the teachers could easily be friends.

For all professors, not only the egotist or narcissist, it is no longer Mr. Jenkins or Ms. Hernandez. Now it is "Doctor" Jenkins or Professor Hernandez. The professor is more formal, class material more theoretical, instructional language more arcane, and teacher-student interaction more proscribed. Even the air feels more rarified. No wonder freshmen enter the classroom with preconceived expectations that many professors will fulfill while others fall far short.

QUESTION

If God accepted a position at a college and university, is it likely that God would be successful?

ANSWER

Not likely. A whole list of problems.

- God had only one major publication, and He did not actually write it himself.
- It was in Hebrew and Aramaic.
- It had no cited references.
- It wasn't submitted for peer review or published in a refereed journal.
- It has not been updated for two thousand years.
- He never applied to the Ethics Board for permission to use human subjects.

PROFESSOR CONTRADICTION

Okay. We have a person of preconceived status who is in a position of total control of our lives or the lives of our children. At the same time, we know that a doctoral degree does not prepare the individual to be a teacher.

> **Student 1.** "Do you like professor Davis?"
> **Student 2.** "No, I don't."
> **Student 1.** "Why?"
> **Student 2.** "Well, he is really smart and he really knows his stuff. He just can't teach."

QUESTION

A posting on a faculty discussion board asked for responses to the following question.

> **Query:** I finished my PhD in a humanities discipline a couple of years ago. I worked for my dissertation adviser as a research assistant before accepting a position as an assistant professor. During my second year of teaching, my adviser published an article based on our work together. He previously indicated I would be named as a co-author but it did not happen.
>
> Recently, he contacted me to help him with a research project that was part of my dissertation. I am working in the same exact area.
>
> He is a prominent person in my field, and I do not know what to do. I do not want him to "steal" my ideas, but I do not want to make an enemy. What should I do?

ANSWER

Every professor must answer the question for himself. Even superstars run out of ideas and can be tempted to take credit for the work of others. How do you protect your own product considering politics? Good question.

GETTING PUBLISHED

The pursuit of tenure and promotion demands scholarship. If your only choice is to write unimportant articles, go ahead. You probably have the experience as most dissertations are quite obscure.

QUESTION

An individual finished her dissertation, graduated, and accepted a position as an assistant professor. She wrote to a colleague and asked, "Can you help me publish my dissertation?" What was the colleague's response?

ANSWER

Don't bother. The dissertation only counts toward initial hiring. Instead create articles from it or start new research.

EVALUATING SERVICE

Service refers to advising, registration, participation on committees, and other non-academic duties at a college or university.

QUESTION

A tenure-track professor decided to excel in service to her university. She said, "I am going to fight for or support changes to greatly improve our teaching and research." Is this good advice?

ANSWER

No. It is horrible. While on the tenure-track, do not try to change anything. Support others on non-controversial points. Serve on committees that are not important. Stay out of efforts to resolve conflicts. You are in pursuit of the honey but do not disturb the bees too early in the day.

It's one thing to be a respected member of the faculty. Is there more? How do you become a superstar? Let's move beyond the confines of the campus. What do we see?

IS THE ACADEMY MEDIOCRISTAN OR EXTREMISTAN?

Nassim Taleb is a New York University professor who identifies two distinct lifestyle choices.

- **Mediocristan.** Most professors live in this area of few extreme successes or failures.
- **Extremistan.** A few lucky ones find rare occurrences to be academic superstars.

QUESTION

A professor wants to write a blockbuster book. Is she living in Mediocristan or Extremistan?

ANSWER

Mediocristan to be sure. Of six hundred thousand books published each year in the United States, the top five hundred account for 50 percent of sales. The odds against success are long. One lucky author, Kathryn Stockett, overcame them. Her 2009 book, *The Help*, was rejected by sixty literary agents before being accepted by a publisher and selling five million copies.

Another way to look at the academy is to recognize "normal" and "extreme" times that correspond roughly to Mediocristan and Extremistan.

- **Normal Times.** Everyday life on the campus. Classes, office hours, and meetings.
- **Extreme Times.** The rare occurrences, sometimes positive, sometimes negative, that break the routine.

For most aspiring professors, higher education is normal times in Mediocristan. The United States has an estimated 1.5 million college and university teachers. Of these, a small number achieve wealth or fame.

PROFESSORS IN EXTREMISTAN

Many "professors" who make it as superstars are outsiders. Among the twenty-five most famous professors on a recent list, ten were famous elsewhere and then joined a college or university:

Name	*School*	*Fame*
Leonard Maltin	University of Southern California	Film critic
Nancy Schiesari	Texas	Filmmaker
Spike Lee	Tisch School	Filmmaker
Dennis Green	San Diego State	Football coach
Maya Angelou	Wake Forest	Poet
Al Gore	Meddle Tennessee	Politician
Jimmy Carter	Emory	Politician
Madeleine Albright	Georgetown	Politician
Jose Maria Anzar	Georgetown	Politician
Jay Craven	Marlboro	Screenwriter

The others were famous for teaching or scholarship:

Name	*School*
Bill Ayers	Illinois
Daniel Johnson	Colorado College
Elinor Ostrom	Indiana
Elliott West	Arkansas
Greg Mankiw	Harvard
Henry Gates Jr.	Harvard
J. Scott Armstrong	Wharton School
Jason Petta	Princeton
Lawrence Lessig	Harvard Law
Michael Liebler	Wayne State
Michael Mann	Penn State
Noam Chomsky	Massachusetts Institute of Technology
Salman Rushdie	Massachusetts Institute of Technology
Temple Grandin	Colorado State
Thomas Steitz	Yale

Universities understand Mediocristan and Extremistan quite well. They seek to hire a few superstars and base their reputations on those individuals.

QUESTION

A university has one hundred professors with average publications in the last five years of 1.5 per professor. They added twenty-five professors with average publications of three. Did the publication profile rise significantly?

ANSWER

No. The effort reflects Mediocristan, as we have no extreme result.

- **Original.** 150 publications
- **Revised.** 225 publications
- **Original.** 1.5 average (1,500/100)
- **Revised.** 1.8 average (225/125)

QUESTION

A department has ten professors with average publications in the last five years of 1.5 per professor. They added one professor with sixty publications. Did the publication profile rise significantly?

ANSWER

Extremistan, as we have a significant, even if meaningless, rise.

- **Original.** Fifteen publications
- **Revised.** Seventy-five publications
- **Original.** 1.5 average (15/10)
- **Revised.** 6.8 average (75/11)

SUPERSTAR PROFESSORS

Everyone has his or her own idea of what it means to be an academic superstar. In 2013, *Business Insider* identified the ten most famous professors teaching college courses. It is a sobering realization for professors that most of these individuals, whatever their teaching credentials, make the list outside the academy and then return to it. In no special order or ranking:

- **Madeleine Albright.** Politician, diplomat, and former U.S. secretary of State. She made the list as a professor of diplomacy in the School of Foreign Service at Georgetown. Student gave her rave reviews. Her PhD is from Columbia.
- **Maya Angelou (deceased).** American poet, memoirist, and civil rights activist who received a lifetime professorship at Wake Forest. She was loved by students.
- **David Brooks.** Senior Fellow at Yale but mainly a columnist for the *New York Times*, a political and cultural commentator, and a renowned author.
- **Junot Diaz.** Dominican American writer, Pulitzer Prize winner, and recipient of a MacArthur Fellowship. A student exclaimed, "a breath of fresh air from the dullness that is usually [Massachusetts Institute of Technology]" (anonymous student quote posted on www.RateMyProfessor.com).
- **Henry Louis Gates Jr.** American literary critic, teacher, historian, filmmaker, and public intellectual as well as professor at Harvard.
- **Temple Grandin.** Professor of animal science at Colorado State University; she is autistic and is a world-renowned autism spokesperson.

- **Paul Krugman.** Professor of economics at the City University of New York, professor emeritus at Princeton, a renowned author and columnist for the *New York Times*, and a Nobel Prize winner.
- **Leonard Maltin.** Taught a film symposium at the University of Southern California. His day job was American film critic, historian, and author.
- **Salman Rushdie.** British Indian novelist and essayist and Distinguished Professor at Emory University.
- **Cornel West.** American philosopher, social activist, author, and professor at the Union Theological Seminary.

PROFESSORIAL CONTROVERSY AND STARDOM

Sometimes superstar status is achieved by controversy. A website identified the ten most controversial college professors in America.

- **Ben Carson.** American retired neurosurgeon, Fox News commentator, political columnist, and 2016 presidential candidate.
- **Noam Chomsky.** American linguist, philosopher, social critic, and political activist who has been called, "one of the most dishonest and dangerous men in America" (David Horowitz, "The sick mind of Noam Chomsky," www.salon.com, September 26, 2011).
- **Robert George.** Professor at Princeton famous for public stands opposing abortion, same-sex marriage, and stem cell research.
- **Mary Ann Glendon.** Professor at Harvard Law whose attacks against Notre Dame helped the sale of her eleven books for scholarly and general audiences.
- **William Happer.** Professor at Princeton who opposed "the demonization of carbon dioxide"in clean air discussions ("CNBC's Climate 'Expert': 'Demonization of Carbon Dioxide Is Just Like' Demonization of 'Jews under Hitler,'" *Media Matters for America*, July 15, 2014).
- **Leon Kass.** University of Chicago professor emeritus whose opposition to embryonic stem cell research brought him both fame and criticism.
- **Catharine MacKinnon.** Professor of law at the University of Michigan and a radical feminist, scholar, and activist.
- **Thomas Nagel.** Professor at New York University who is controversial because he challenged Darwin's theory in the creation versus evolution debate.
- **Peter Singer.** Professor at Princeton University whose perspective on applied economics seems to abandon the disadvantaged and less fortunate.
- **Thomas Sowell.** Economist at Stanford University who claims affirmative action harms blacks, whites, Asians, and Hispanics.

PROFESSOR JAMES LANG AND TEACHING SUPERSTARS

Every now and then we realize that places exist for professors who simply want to teach. James Lang, a professor at Assumption College, made this point in an article in the *Chronicle of Higher Education*.

He encountered a bright student who wanted to pursue a PhD. When Lang learned the student could not afford the cost of an entrance exam, he sent the provost an email describing the situation and asked for the college to help. The response of the provost? "Of course, we could help." The student is now pursuing a PhD.

Professor Lang uses the story to argue for the value of teaching at community, liberal arts, and regional colleges. He observes the satisfaction of offering "the miracle of education" to first-generation college students working to improve their lives.

QUESTION

Does Professor Lang believe a faculty career at a teaching-intensive college is superior one to a research university?

ANSWER

No. He actually praises researchers in his field and claims "scholars fully deserve the credits and accolades that attach to their work" (James M. Lang, "Why You Might Love Working at a Teaching College," *Chronicle of Higher Education*, October 30, 2016).

QUESTION

Professor Lang was promoted to associate professor in 2006 and full professor in 2013. Why did it take so long? I sent him an email:

> According to your biography, it took seven years to move from associate to full professor. With all your professional achievements, this seems a little long. Does it reflect a bias in favor of refereed-journal articles as opposed to scholarship focusing on teaching?

Did he reply?

ANSWER

He responded the next day.

> The only reason I did not move from associate to full more quickly was pure laziness on my part. I was concentrating on writing my books and, as I'm sure you know, putting together that application packet is a colossal task.

QUESTION

Can Professor Lang do anything to improve his "lazy ways"? Does he simply not care about being a superstar?

ANSWER

He is certainly not lazy. Maybe he is a superstar. He lectures all over the place. He has multiple publications, including books published by Harvard University Press and Johns Hopkins Press.

QUESTION

As a teaching "superstar," has Professor Lang joined the ranks of Madeleine Albright or Maya Angelou?

ANSWER

Not according to Wikipedia, where the only James Lang is a six-foot nine-inch, 315-pound professional basketball player whose fame derives from playing basketball for nine different teams for parts of six active seasons.

QUESTION

Does James Lang live in Mediocristan or Extremistan?

ANSWER

It appears that one James Lang lives in each area.

A DISMAL PROJECTION FOR THE FUTURE

The term "adjunctification" began to appear in the *Chronicle* sometime around the year 2000. In 2017, it was not recognized by either the Oxford or Merriam-Webster dictionaries.

It refers to the process of increasingly using adjunct professors instead of tenure-track faculty. Critics define it as the academy's "overreliance" on part-time faculty.

Kevin Birmingham, adjunct instructor in the Harvard College Writing Program and Truman Capote Award winner, says the adjunctification of the humanities represents "the great shame of our profession." He argues the creation of "elite faculty positions" forces universities to rely upon a "revolving door of new PhDs who work temporarily for unsustainable wages and then disappear, being replaced by next year's surplus doctorates" (Kevin Birmingham, "Truman Capote Award Acceptance Speech," *Chronicle of Higher Education*, October 19, 2016).

If Birmingham is right, the academic Mediocristan is worse than we thought. If you succeed in reaching superstardom, what are you? According to Dr. Birmingham:

> If you are a tenured . . . faculty member teaching in a humanities department with Ph.D. candidates, you are both the instrument and the direct beneficiary of exploitation. Your roles as teacher, adviser, and committee member generate, cultivate, and exploit young people's devotion to literature.

This dismal assessment does not, of course, refer to the professors who toil without graduate assistants to deliver the lessons of the liberal arts.

CONCLUSION AND FALLACIES

Like everything else in a media-intensive world, the pathway to academic superstardom is littered with debris. Professors live in Mediocristan and hope somehow to teach or publish to break out of the pack. Success with students may create unknown superstars, the professors who make a difference in the lives of their students. Others may not care so much. Hence:

Fallacy 10. Society recognizes and respects professors who share lessons in the liberal arts.

Reality 10. Liberal arts professors achieve recognition and respect mostly from their students and nowhere else.

Chapter Eleven

Do Professors Need Both Cognitive and Emotional Intelligence? If We Understand the Great Ideas, Why Do We Need More?

> When dealing with people, remember you are not dealing with creatures of logic, but with creatures of emotion.
>
> —Dale Carnegie, writer and lecturer

PROFESSOR SIMANEK'S CHALLENGE TO ACADEMIC INSTITUTIONS

Colleges and universities deal with "the development of the mind." Donald Simanek, a professor from Lock Haven University, claimed this is no longer the case. A broader, more permissive view is the academy has come to mean "anything that occurs in a school" (Donald E. Simanek, "The Decline of Education 2," online blog at https://www.lhup.edu/~dsimanek/decline2.htm).

The goal of Plato's Academy and medieval university was to develop mental powers. The task of forming values and the socialization of citizens occurred in the family or community.

Those days are long gone according to Simanek. Colleges and universities accept responsibility for the "development of the whole individual," covering anything society needs that is not being addressed elsewhere.

Remedial English and mathematics as formal college subjects are just the start of the process. We can hardly make the distinction between academic and non-academic activities.

Simanek argues that we should "drastically clean the academic house." He points out, as an example, you do not need an education to become a concert pianist. You do need skill but creating it is not the job of the college teacher. His view is that higher education should be limited to "mathematics, natural sciences, and some parts of philosophy" (Donald E. Simanek, "The Decline of Education 2," online blog at https://www.lhup.edu/~dsimanek/decline2.htm). Plus, of course, a good library.

Lest it seem we have a quarrel with Professor Simanek, he recommends rethinking the "standard four-year curriculum." Many students do not need it. He also believes "far fewer people" should attend universities than do now and many universities should be "converted to other worthy purposes" (ibid.).

QUESTION

Hypothetically, Plato invited Ghengis, a brilliant young scholar to teach a course at the Academy. He knew every theory and concept related to warfare in the ancient world. He was ruthlessly crude and ill-mannered. How do you think he did with his students?

ANSWER

I think Profession Simanek would agree the answer is not well. Interpersonal relations are needed in communication about philosophy and other academic subjects. Perhaps fewer people should go to traditional colleges but those who go need interpersonal skills and strong value systems to succeed with whatever knowledge they gain.

COGNITIVE INTELLIGENCE

An IQ test measures a person's ability to think, reason, and remember. This is called cognitive intelligence, a general mental capability to reason, solve problems, and understand complex ideas. It differs from emotional intelligence, the ability to identify and manage your own emotions and the emotions of others.

Cognitive intelligence measured by IQ is supposed to have a median score of one hundred. It varies widely around the world. In one research study, Hong Kong, Singapore, and South Korea have a median of 108; China and Japan are 105; and European nations tend to range from 98 to 102. The United States, at 98, is four points higher than Kazakhstan, Romania, and Vietnam.

IQ scores between 90 and 110 are considered average. Over 120 is superior. Two-thirds of the world's people are in the range of 85 to 115. Between 70 and 130 we find 95 percent of the world's population.

INTELLIGENCE AND EMOTIONAL QUOTIENT

Many liberal arts disciplines deal with human behavior. We recognize two basic orientations.

- **Intelligence Quotient (IQ).** A measure of intelligence derived by comparing "mental age" to a person's actual age in years. We use IQ tests to measure potential educational achievement or predict job performance.
- **Emotional Quotient (EQ).** The capacity to understand one's own emotions and those of others. Individuals are judged on their ability to identify, assess, and manage the emotions of themselves and others.

QUESTION

With respect to perceptions, thinking, meaning, and management of emotions, does cognitive or emotional intelligence have the edge?

ANSWER

Emotional intelligence. It more accurately identifies situations, facilitates moving from feelings and opinions to facts and beliefs, seeks to understand hidden messages, and can better manage interaction with others.

QUESTION

An advanced degree places a premium on cognitive intelligence in an undergraduate classroom. In terms of teaching and helping others, does an emphasis on cognitive intelligence make sense?

ANSWER

Emotional intelligence has an edge:

- **Perceptions.** Emotional intelligence can more accurately identify emotions.
- **Thinking.** Emotional intelligence facilitates moving from feelings and opinions to facts and beliefs.

- **Meaning.** Emotional intelligence seeks to understand hidden messages.
- **Management.** Emotional intelligence can better manage the emotions of others.

QUESTION

Can an individual increase his or her cognitive or emotional intelligence?

ANSWER

Most researchers believe IQ is stable over time and cannot be changed. They are mixed on EQ. Some argue it is static. Some say it is dynamic.

QUESTION

Do people exhibit more IQ or EQ behavior in their daily lives?

ANSWER

For most people, the answer depends on past personal experiences. Both behaviors at the extreme are common.

LIBERAL ARTS AND BEHAVIOR

The liberal arts address both IQ and EQ. The fields of philosophy, psychology, sociology, history, and geography would almost be devoid of content without EQ. We would be lost understanding Russia if we did not study emotions in the court of the czars, and we would have no clue about what happened in the 2016 presidential race if we did not incorporate EQ into the discussion.

CONCLUSION AND FALLACIES

In the pursuit of knowledge, an important component is an understanding of the context of knowledge. To use information in critical thinking is one thing.

To convert it into effective behavior requires emotional intelligence. Liberal arts help students apply evidence to current events in their lives. Hence:

Fallacy 11. A doctoral degree from a recognized school is the proper preparation for teaching the liberal arts.
Reality 11. Professors need both cognitive and emotional intelligence to effectively share the full capabilities of the liberal arts.

Chapter Twelve

Can Professors Help Us Improve Decision Making? If We Only Know the Theory, Is That Enough?

In theory there is no difference between theory and practice. In practice, there is.

—Yogi Berra, American baseball player

RATIONAL BEHAVIOR

Our basis for understanding how people make choices starts with models of social and economic behavior. Economics 101 tells us individuals have preferences among available alternatives and can rank them. If option A is preferred over option B and option B is preferred over option C, then A is preferred over C. This is known as rational choice theory.

The theory assumes people take account of available information, likelihood of events, and costs and benefits of each option, and then choose the best choice of behavior to meet their needs.

Does rational choice theory work? Let's take a look.

STRATEGIC AND SITUATIONAL DECISION MAKING

We can identify two kinds of decisions:

- **Strategic Decisions.** We display strategic skills when we solve problems and make correct choices.
- **Situational Decisions.** We show situational skills when we adjust our activities to respond to changing circumstances.

JÜRGEN SCHREMPP AT DAIMLER BENZ

A story about the 1998 Daimler Benz acquisition of Chrysler illustrates the difference between strategic and situational decision making. Jürgen Schrempp, chief executive officer of Daimler Benz, described the deal as "a merger of equals, a merger of growth, and a merger of unprecedented strength" ("DaimlerChrysler dawns: Board stuns auto world with $38B merger; biggest cross-border deal ever," CNN Money, May 7, 1998). In the next years, problems arose.

In late 2000, it was war. Jürgen Schrempp said to a German newspaper that he always intended Chrysler to be a subsidiary of DaimlerChrysler. He continued, "The merger-of-equals statement was necessary to earn the support of Chrysler's workers and the American public, but it was never reality" (ibid.).

QUESTION

Does the behavior of Mr. Schrempp show any elements of cognitive or emotional intelligence?

ANSWER

Not really. It also shows two failures.

- **Strategic Decision.** The "merger" with Chrysler, with no plans to merge cultures, was a failure of strategy.
- **Situational Decision.** The 2000 statement that he lied in 1998 was a bad situational decision by Mr. Schrempp.

QUESTION

How did it turn out for the merger?

ANSWER

Not good for Daimler. It paid $37 billion to acquire Chrysler. In 2007, it sold 80 percent of Chrysler to Cerberus, a private equity firm, for $7 billion.

FedEx MOVES, SHOOTS, AND COMMUNICATES

FedEx offers us another lesson in behavior. Rob Carter, the chief information officer at FedEx, was asked, "What business are you in?" One possible answer would be that FedEx is in the business of shipping or package delivery. That makes sense as the company shipped six million packages a day in 2006. It had 39 hubs in 180 countries, ran 677 airplanes and 9,000 vehicles, and employed 200,000 people.

Rob Carter answered, "FedEx engineers time." He was reflecting the view of Fred Smith, FedEx chief executive officer and founder. He saw things in the big picture. FedEx offers solutions to allow customers to make things happen on time schedules that otherwise would be impossible.

QUESTION

FedEx spent billions of dollars so customers could track any individual FedEx shipment using the Internet. Does this reflect cognitive or emotional intelligence?

ANSWER

Both. FedEx gave customers the ability to see every inbound package even if they did not know it was coming. They accompanied this information with an obsession to prevent packages from being lost, damaged, or delayed. These behaviors facilitated efficient processing as well as dealing with any anxieties about the location of incoming packages.

QUESTION

A medical laboratory tests samples of bone marrow in advance of its use by hospitals in surgeries. When does it learn how many such tests will need to be performed tomorrow?

ANSWER

It learns immediately when the shipment moves by FedEx. By tracking every inbound shipment sent today, a laboratory can schedule enough technicians to test all samples tomorrow. FedEx notifies the laboratory of shipments on the way.

QUESTION

As an undergraduate, Fred Smith wrote a paper outlining overnight delivery service in a computer information age. What happened to his class submission?

ANSWER

The professor gave the paper a grade of "C." He decided the idea to compete with the U.S. Post Office was not feasible. We do not know how he came to this conclusion. Nor do we know if he subsequently changed the grade.

QUESTION

How does the story of FedEx link to the goals of the liberal arts?

ANSWER

It shows the importance of being able to think beyond narrow boundaries. "FedEx engineers time"? That sounds like the viewpoint of someone who studied in the academy. Maybe it was. Fred Smith, an economics undergraduate major at Yale University.

FORD AND FIRESTONE RECALL

To illustrate the failure of situational decision making, we can examine a crisis that occurred in the year 2000. The U.S. government told Ford and Firestone about tire failure on Ford Explorers. Blowouts of Firestone tires caused a series of accidents causing 250 deaths and 3,000 serious injuries.

The story made international news and put massive pressure on Firestone to recall the tires and Ford to encourage owners to replace them. After a week of blistering media attention, Firestone announced a recall of seven million tires, offering to replace all affected tires without question.

Neither Ford nor Firestone was prepared for the media damage. They fought bitterly in the press, each denying fault and blaming the other for the accidents. They responded to questions with daily missives to the news media and took a full week to respond to the crisis. The decision makers at both companies seemed unable to devise an effective strategy to reduce the damage.

QUESTION

What happened because of the media battle?

ANSWER

After more than one week, the two companies realized the damage that had been done. They made every effort to produce and distribute replacement tires and mount them on Ford vehicles. Ford took a hit to its image, earnings, and stock price. Firestone experienced even more severe problems. The media created an image of Firestone as a company that produced questionable products. The sale of Firestone tires dropped 30 percent and the value of its stock was cut in half. The company reported a loss of $750 million in 2000.

LIBERAL ARTS DECISION MAKING

Could a recent graduate with a liberal arts foundation accurately size up the problem facing Ford and Firestone? One possible answer:

- **Strategic Decision.** Neither company had the right structure to respond to the crisis. Time was wasted with strategy sessions at high levels to formulate a course of action for the crisis.
- **Situational Decision.** There was no way to win a slugfest in the media. The companies were communicating the wrong messages.

If we are doing it right with undergraduates, they learn decision making occurs as a combination in cognitive and emotional intelligence. The liberal arts should teach us to exhibit wide latitude including:

- **Acknowledge the Upside.** A lost opportunity is a form of risk. To fail to decide can be a mistake if we miss an opportunity.

- **Remember our Goal.** Every decision should move us closer to our objective.
- **Recognize What is Important.** What are the strengths and weaknesses of our position? What are the priorities, benefits, and risks of different courses of action?

QUESTION

A guest in a hotel lost an earring. She approaches a doorman to help find it. He points out that he cannot leave the entrance to the hotel. Is this a good decision?

ANSWER

Not necessarily. The theory is an employee must follow the rules forbidding leaving a post. The reality is to do something to give the guest a good feeling leading to future business.

QUESTION

A guest orders special flowers for her room and pays for them during a visit. A year later, she arrives for another visit. She finds the same kind of flowers in her room. Is this a good decision?

ANSWER

It looks like it. A manager with a liberal arts background might know good things happen when the staff anticipates needs and is thoughtful.

QUESTION

For decision making, what should a liberal arts foundation encourage?

ANSWER

Exceed expectations. Make decisions and take actions to share a vision, create your own pathway, follow up on expectations, and pick your battles.

QUESTION

A hospital is constructing a new modern facility. How would a person with a liberal arts background explain it to a manager, an analyst, a skeptic, and a leader?

ANSWER

- **Manager.** We are building a new facility to improve efficiency.
- **Analyst.** Our new hospital is cost-effective.
- **Skeptic.** We may not really need a new facility but here it is.
- **Leader.** Our new facility is another sign of why we are the leader in health care.

QUESTION

Should the liberal arts warn us about decisions on rainy days?

ANSWER

Yes. Never make a big decision when conditions distract or dismay you.

- **Lawyer on Steps of Courthouse**. "I am having a bad day. We'll just have to hope that the jury does not convict you and vote for the death sentence."
- **Doctor before Surgery.** "I am having a bad day. We'll just have to hope that I remember to connect all the arteries after your heart transplant."

QUESTION

In the late 1990s, Nokia developed a prototype of the Apple iPhone of 2007. It had a color touch screen. It could play games and order retail products. It did not ever make it to market. What would liberal arts training tell us about this?

ANSWER

Figure out what is happening. As it turns out, the engineers at Nokia wanted to build the technology they knew instead of responding to the needs of customers. The company spent billions on research while lagging behind Apple and Samsung throughout the first decade of the twenty-first century.

QUESTION

A boss called a vice president into her office and told him a key employee had offended the wife of the chief executive officer of the company. It happened at a community function not related to work. She instructed the vice president to fire the individual and said the order was not negotiable. The vice president refused to follow the order. Was this a good move?

ANSWER

Who knows? This shows the limits of making decisions without enough information. Liberal arts thinking would be to recognize that following the order may be wrong. Refusing to follow it may be worse.

QUESTION

Assume you have three candidates for a job. Who would be your first choice to hire?

- **"A."** Would be spectacular at the job. He has some personality issues and is expensive to hire.
- **"B."** Would be competent at the job. She is well liked and is available at the budget number.
- **"C."** Would be more than competent at the job. He is also well liked and is available a little above the budget number.

ANSWER

Whatever the answer, a liberal arts graduate might be prepared to tell them:

- Average results are not good enough.
- Great things come from a diverse workforce.
- We want motivated people who do great work.
- We expect people to be high performers.

QUESTION

A primary stakeholder in an organization is someone who makes it successful. Of the president, dean, professors, students, or staff, who is the primary stakeholder for a liberal arts college?

ANSWER

Arguably, it is the professors. When they take care of the students, everything else tends to work out.

LIBERAL ARTS AND CRITICAL THINKING

One challenge facing professors when young people arrive for their freshman year is that many high schools did not encourage critical thinking. Even the best high schools tend to emphasize information to the exclusion of challenging the truth. Read the textbooks. Achieve good grades and high scores on standardized exams. You did it. Welcome to college.

When the student reaches Plato's modern academy, professors attempt to build critical-thinking skills. We know what this means:

- **Interpretation.** Understand and explain information to others.
- **Analysis.** Connect pieces of information into a meaningful pattern.
- **Inference.** Follow logical reasoning steps moving from premises to conclusions.
- **Evaluation.** Recognize the validity of statements, descriptions, experiences, judgments, and opinions.
- **Explanation.** Communicate information to others augmented by your own clarity and perspective.

- **Self-Regulation.** Recognize strengths and limitations in your own thinking abilities as you draw conclusions or decide on a course of action.

When the liberal arts are successful, students internalize knowledge useful for making decisions:

- **Untruths Aren't Always Lies.** A person who deliberately misrepresents what he or she knows to be true is lying. Someone unaware of the facts or in denial about them is not lying. He or she is simply stating a falsehood.
- **People Distort Reality.** Everybody distorts reality along a scale stretching from mild to severe. Minor distortions cause odd decisions. Delusions can produce totally irrational thoughts and actions.
- **Falsehoods are a Fact of Life.** Mistruths are voiced by normal people all the time and do not indicate the presence of a psychiatric disorder. People have false memories. A friend can be certain he or she mailed you an invitation to a wedding when, in fact, he or she never did.
- **Some People are Pathological Liars.** It can be hard for undergraduates to accept the presence of people who prefer to lie rather than tell the truth. Whatever their motivations, a critical component of critical thinking is to recognize the behavior and deal with it effectively.
- **People Abuse the Facts.** Facts are used to support beliefs in a variety of ways. They give people a basis for, a need to, or an excuse to reach a conclusion. They abuse facts to defend a decision that does not work out. Students need to learn that someone will give them a belief when they demand, "Give me the facts."

QUESTION

Distinguishing the truth has always been a goal of the liberal arts. Why discuss it now?

ANSWER

Society has experienced an explosive increase in knowledge accompanied by a revolution in communications and the sharing of information. We are experiencing a breakdown in decision making based on misleading information. American University professor Charles Lewis captures the urgency of addressing the problem in his book, *935 Lies: The Future of Truth and the Decline of America's Moral Integrity*. The book documents government misinformation leading up to the 2003 Iraq War. Subsequent events, including the 2016 presidential elections, showed the general public had an appetite for falsehood.

QUESTION

This is a staggering problem. What can professors do about it?

ANSWER

Students need to recognize the widespread behavioral distortions and be prepared to deal with them. A renewal of the liberal arts with a stronger sense of urgency can help.

CONCLUSION AND FALLACIES

The link between the liberal arts and decision making has a long history in the United States, Canada, and beyond. Effective politicians and social and business leaders often come from liberal arts colleges. They reflect upon strategic decisions, are not distracted by situational changes that produce crises, and help us prepare for survival in a complex and changing world. But a new reality has emerged. Hence:

Fallacy 12. Liberal arts provide the knowledge needed to make good decisions.

Reality 12. Liberal arts should intensify its efforts to encourage seeking evidence and applying critical thinking to help us make better decisions.

Part IV

RESTRUCTURING THE CURRICULUM

Chapter Thirteen

Why Should Professors Encourage Students to Take Chances? What Good Things Might Happen if We Leave Our Comfort Zones?

Whatever you do, don't mention risk management. It is so boring.

—Doreen Tango Hampton, upon learning that her husband had been invited to speak at an insurance industry conference

The liberal arts do not teach us how to build, repair, and modify people, buildings, or financial statements. They encourage us to assess risk using evidence, not beliefs. How are we doing?

CHINESE VIEW OF RISK

Most of us think of risk as being something that can harm us. "I won't ride a horse. I could get hurt." Risk, in our everyday view, is a negative. The Merriam-Webster dictionary defines risk as the possibility that something bad or unpleasant will happen. It refers to injury or loss. It is exposure to a danger or hazard.

The Chinese had a more sophisticated understanding of the concept. In the written Chinese language, the character for "risk" or "crisis" combines the characters of "danger" and "opportunity." Risk has an upside as well as a downside.

Chinese linguists point out that the character does not actually signify "opportunity." Instead, it means a specific moment when something begins or changes. In a risky situation, the outcome can be better or worse than expected. If this is not both danger and opportunity, what is it?

FEAR OF FLYING

Pteromerhanophobia, aerophobia, aviatophobia, or aviophobia are four terms that refer to the fear of flying in an airplane. Some 40 percent of Americans have anxiety about boarding an airplane, and one adult in four refuses to fly under any circumstances. Others medicate themselves in order to fly. Are these behaviors rational given the following information?

- Deaths per one hundred million passengers:
  - 1962–1971: 133 deaths
  - 2001–2017: 2 deaths
- Annual global passengers:
  - 1960: 106 million
  - 2016: 3.6 billion
- Odds of dying:
  - In a crash in the United States: one in twenty-nine million
  - From a lightning strike: one in eleven million
  - While riding a bicycle: one in 340,000

Many people do not want to hear about how safe it is to fly. They would ignore information showing three fatal crashes, 118 deaths, among 190 million U.S. commercial flights from 2002 to 2016. Nor would it be helpful to point out that thirty-five thousand people a year die in auto accidents, including fifty or so in taxis taking people to airports.

The safety of air travel can be seen in the list of U.S. carrier crashes with fatalities between 2000 and 2016:

Table 13.1.

Year	*Airline*	*Location*	*Fatalities*
2009	Continental Commuter	Buffalo, NY	48
2006	Delta Connection	Lexington, KY	49
2003	US Air Commuter	Charlotte, NC	21
2001	American Airlines	New York, NY	260
2001	American Airlines	New York, NY	87
2001	United Airlines	New York, NY	60
2001	American Airlines	Washington, DC	59
2001	United Airlines	Pittsburgh, PA	41
2000	Alaska Airlines	Los Angeles, CA	88

With respect to our assessment of risk, beliefs overcome data and common sense. This is the case for individuals as well as the organizations they join.

QUESTION

Three insurance policies can be purchased for the same price at an airport covering the loss of life connected to an upcoming flight.

- A life insurance policy pays $10,000.
- An accidental death insurance policy pays $10,000.
- A terrorism death insurance policy pays $10,000.

Which policy is most attractive to individuals preparing to fly?

ANSWER

We should not be surprised if the terrorism policy provokes an overreaction and is the best seller, even though the other two policies cover terrorism-related death plus other accidental death.

QUESTION

A corporation has a policy that no three of its ten senior executives can travel together on the same flight on one of the fifteen major U.S. carriers. Is this a sound risk management strategy?

ANSWER

With an average of forty-five thousand flights per day and one fatal crash every forty million or so commercial flights, the executives could fly together every day for fifteen hundred years before being involved in a fatal crash.

Having assessed flight safety, liberal arts training encourages us to avoid overconfidence. Could the situation change? Probably not, but we might watch out for:

- Failure of automated cockpit systems
- Cyber attacks

- Pilot fatigue and other human factors
- Bird strikes and collisions with drones
- Greater turbulence from climate change

BROADEN THE PERSPECTIVE OF RISK

Liberal arts encourage critical assessment of new possibilities. We have stories to help us change our view of risk.

QUESTION

In the late 1990s, Ford Motor Corporation was dealing with a possible disruption of future production. The rare metal palladium was the key component in catalytic converters. Its sources of supply were unstable. To avoid production delays, the purchasing department signed long-term contracts to guarantee a supply of palladium. Did the strategy work to reduce this risk?

ANSWER

No. Ford's research and development department recognized the same exposure. The result was a redesigned catalytic converter that did not require the rare metal. Other manufacturers followed, causing the price per ounce of palladium to drop from $1,500 to $400. In 2002, Ford cancelled the contract, suffering a $1 billion penalty.

QUESTION

Tata, India's largest automobile company, offered the Tata Nano in 2009 with a starting price of $2,200. The company worried about who would be potential customers as economists believed Indians were becoming more prosperous and wanted bigger, not smaller, cars. Were they right?

ANSWER

Yes, but Tata expanded its thinking. It discovered a population segment of families who used motorcycles to transport entire families and small businesses that used them for deliveries. It designed and offered the simplest possible car. More than a motorcycle and a $700 price. If you buy the small Tata, be prepared to have one windshield wiper instead of two, no tubes in your tire, and no radio.

QUESTION

A retailer was negotiating the purchase of a grocery chain. The goal was to upgrade the acquired locations to the more modern standards of the company's own stores. The business plan made sense. At the last minute, the company asked, "Do we have all the evidence we need?" To answer the question, they sent people to visit the stores to be acquired. What did they find?

ANSWER

Asbestos used as insulation in the walls. Renovating the stores would activate a hazardous materials requirement to remediate an entire store. This costly discovery changed the deal and caused the company to renegotiate the price it would pay to buy the stores.

MANAGE INFORMATION: HURRICANE ANDREW

Critical thinking encourages us to challenge the things we think we know. Hurricanes offer this opportunity.

QUESTION

In 1992, Hurricane Andrew caused significant losses for insurance companies, much more than it should have been. Why did this happen?

ANSWER

Another failure of critical thinking. Florida insurance law did not distinguish flood and wind damage. Different insurance policies cover wind and water damage. When a homeowner had only one coverage, which policy paid for a destroyed home? Did the wind take off the roof before a storm surge leveled the house? Lawsuits were costly to sort out who reimbursed losses.

QUESTION

A second Hurricane Andrew story reveals a flaw in data. Insurance premiums were based on hurricane losses. Florida had no hurricanes for many years, so losses and premiums were low. What was the mistake?

ANSWER

It was a belief in obsolete data based on a 1928 hurricane. In the 1920s, houses were built with masonry walls and clay tile roofs. Both withstood wind damage very well. In the 1980s, houses were not so well constructed. They had asphalt roofs connected to the walls with nails or staples. Hurricanes were getting stronger as the Atlantic Ocean had grown warmer. The forecast data was based on what happened, not mostly on what will happen.

QUESTION

Did the absence of critical thinking seriously harm any of the insurance companies?

ANSWER

Yes. Eleven of them went bankrupt.

CONCLUSION AND FALLACIES

A criticism of liberal arts is that it does not prepare graduates for life after college. Nothing could be further from the truth. Knowledge gained in a proper liberal arts framework encourages to take calculated risks. Hence:

Fallacy 13. Liberal arts do not prepare students for employment after college.
Reality 13. Critical thinking helps accurately assess risk and opportunity when making decisions including career choices.

Chapter Fourteen

What's the Big Deal about Context in a Liberal Arts Education? Can't We Just Talk for Seventy-Five Minutes or So?

> The key to good decision making is not knowledge. It is understanding. We are swimming in the former. We are desperately lacking in the latter.
>
> —Malcolm Gladwell, American author

CONTEXT OF THE ACADEMY

Professor Donald Simanek once wrote, "I know a university that offers a course in kitsch, the schlock art that art historians have traditionally ignored as beneath their contempt. But now such 'art' is displayed in . . . art museums, and 'learned' books are written about it. Are we unwilling to make any academic distinctions any more?" (Donald E. Simanek, "What is the meaning of 'academic'?" posted at https://lhup.edu/~dsimanek/academic.htm, undated).

QUESTION

Does a university really offer a course in "kitsch"?

ANSWER

Not exactly. Kitsch is defined as art or design considered to be in poor taste because of excessive garishness or sentimentality, but sometimes appreciated in an ironic or knowing way.Simanek apparently refers to "German 011 Bad Taste," offered by the University of Pennsylvania. With a degree in physics from Penn State, he was poking fun at the academy, as has been his wont to do for many years.

Professor Simanek makes a serious point in his essay. He points out that "academic" once meant "pertaining to the development of the mind." Now, he says, it means "anything that occurs in a school" (Donald E. Simanek, "What is the meaning of 'academic'?" posted at https://lhup.edu/~dsimanek/academic.htm, undated).

He seems to long for a return to Plato's Academy where it was not the job of the professors to instill social skills, teach good health practices, promote drug education, or offer courses in safe driving.

Simanek is talking about the context of higher education. The goal of education should be the "development of mental powers to the exclusion of everything else." The teaching of values, ethics, and the general socialization of the individual should be "left to the home and community" (ibid.).

Thus, we introduce the importance of context. It affects everything else we do and is a major concern of any effort to think critically.

CONTEXT OF THE LIBERAL ARTS

Professor Simanek is not alone in his view of the academy. Neither is he the most vocal voice. If you ask Google to give you the "benefits of a liberal arts degree," you will get twelve or more pages of guidance. The liberal arts prepare you to work in a variety of areas, introduces you to career choice, is a stepping-stone to other careers, is appealing to employers, provides a foundation for graduate study, and gives you skills to become a valuable community member.

Without further engaging in the valid context of the liberal arts, let's address teaching students the importance of context.

CONTEXT AND TIPPING POINTS

Malcolm Gladwell contributed many liberal arts ideas in four books, namely *Outliers*, *Blink*, *The Tipping Point*, and most recently *David and Goliath*. Two of his concepts are particularly powerful.

- **Context.** This is a situation in which something happens. It is a critical variable that affects our behavior.

- **Tipping Point.** This is the point at which a series of small changes or incidents becomes significant enough to cause a larger, more important change.

Gladwell documented the importance of context and phenomenon of tipping points as key factors for achieving our goals. First, we cover context.

GENETICS OR ENVIRONMENT?

Proponents of a liberal arts education sometimes become embroiled in a controversy as to whether leaders are born or created. It is an age-old question. Perhaps, it is the wrong question. The real issue is whether someone exhibits the right behavior in a specific situation.

In Gladwell's language, we are, "exquisitely sensitive to our environment, past experiences, and current situation" (Malcolm Gladwell, *The Tipping Point: How Little Things Can Make a Big Difference*, New York: Little Brown, and Company, 2000). He makes his point dramatically with the next story. It works well for students to discuss the context surrounding Mr. Goetz.

BERNHARD GOETZ IN THE NEW YORK SUBWAY

The time was the 1980s. The subway in New York City was in bad shape. People misbehaved, jumping turnstiles rather than paying fares. Panhandlers demanded money from riders, and petty criminals threatened riders.

In 1984, Bernhard Goetz boarded a train with twenty people in his car. Four young thugs hassled him for money. He shot them all, firing an extra bullet into one of them, Darrell Cabey, paralyzing him for life. When the train stopped, Goetz walked away. A week later, he turned himself in to the authorities.

Why did Goetz shoot the men? According to Gladwell, it is the power of context. Violence is contagious in circumstances that allow threatening or violent misbehavior.

The Goetz shooting caused a national incident. One youth had a prior arrest for armed robbery. Another had an arrest for theft. Three of them carried screwdrivers in their pockets. Goetz became a national hero to many people. In 1987, he was acquitted of attempted murder. He served eight months for carrying an unregistered weapon. In a civil lawsuit in 1996, Darrell Cabey was awarded $43 million in damages.

QUESTION

How does the power of context explain the actions of Bernhard Goetz?

ANSWER

- New York at height of crime spree
- Subway platform dimly lit with graffiti on walls
- Subway car floors littered with trash and walls filled with graffiti
- Heat not working well in the subway car
- Poorly maintained tracks slowing down trains

QUESTION

In 1990, new management took over the policing of New York City subways, and they were determined to stop the criminal activity. Where did it start?

ANSWER

It started with context. The effort began by eliminating graffiti and turnstile violations under the theory of "broken windows."

- Stop the breakage of windows in abandoned houses.
- Stop the graffiti.
- The harassment on the street goes down.
- Vandalism stops.
- Petty crimes stop.
- Serious crimes stop.

New York City police arrested turnstile violators and forced "graffiti artists" to spend tens of hours of community service cleaning graffiti off subway cars. Soon small and large misbehaviors and crimes dropped dramatically.

Epilogue. An ancillary benefit occurred. The police checked the background of the minor violators. One out of seven had an outstanding warrant for another crime. One out of twenty was carrying an illegal weapon. Insignificant quality-of-life crimes were the tipping point for violent crime.

ROLLINS COLLEGE

Separately from the importance of context taught to students, the academy itself deals with context.

Disputes often arise. This happened in 2013 when Lewis Duncan, president, proposed a change in the context of education at Rollins College. He described online learning as a viable replacement for traditional courses.

QUESTION

The faculty response was negative, resulting in a vote of no confidence in Mr. Duncan's leadership. Faculty leaders argued that the change would undermine the liberal arts character of the school. Are they right?

ANSWER

Whatever your answer, the discussion is totally a dispute about context. Do colleges really need to make dramatic changes in the context of the liberal arts? As with all things, time will tell.

NAVY SEALS TO THE RESCUE

Creating the right context for danger and intensity is another important lesson. The Navy Sea Air Land teams, Navy SEALs in short, pay attention to context. Elements:

- **Loyalty.** One for all and all for one. Lead by example and give unconditional support to others.
- **Team Value Added.** Focus on your goals and make decisions that increase the chance to achieve them. Everybody and every decision adds value.
- **Learn from Your Mistakes.** What did we do? Why did it fail? What will we do next time?
- **Organize Your World.** Identify what must be done to accomplish a goal. Arrange the steps and priorities in a strategy to succeed.
- **Avoid Overconfidence.** Be confident when deciding. Stop at that point. You are never finished learning. Those who assume they know everything make bad decisions.
- **Watch the Details.** Attention to detail saves lives and leads to success. A lack of attention to detail can derail even the best strategy.

CONTEXT OF UNDERGRADUATE EDUCATION

The lecture method of teaching was never the best approach. Plato in the Academy, the masters in the medieval university, and the most effective teachers in modern universities never relied upon it. Engaging in interactive discussions, great teachers always asked students to do something as part of learning.

Yes, the "masters" introduced knowledge by speaking to the whole group but they did not speak for fifteen weeks, three days a week, for one hour, interrupted only by a multiple choice or handwritten essay exam. They did not address a room filled with eight hundred people taking notes to be engaged later by inexperienced and often unmotivated discussion leaders.

Neither did the Academy transmit knowledge in isolated intellectual silos. It did not value obscure scholarship over interaction with students. The preparation did not isolate masters' candidates in ancient texts for years before engaging them with novitiates.

Even if we could get everybody to understand the value of a liberal arts education, we would have to acknowledge weaknesses in the context of delivering the message.

CONTEXT OF GRADUATE EDUCATION

At the graduate level, context is even more frustrating. Doctoral candidates spend many extra years in education that do not prepare them to be professors. Let's make a short list of things that shape context:

- **Many Candidate, Many Failures.** The road to a doctoral degree is littered with debris. As many as 75 percent of starting candidates fail to finish. The "all-but-dissertation" nomenclature is not a degree. It can be a disaster.
- **Many Applicants, Few Openings.** If one hundred people apply for one tenure-track opening, you might as well buy lottery tickets for a chance to succeed.
- **Many Applicants, Fake Opening.** Many searches are made to comply with outdated university recruiting practices. A powerful person in the process has a "favorite." After a nationwide search, the school announces, "We found the most qualified candidate." Really?
- **Interviewing Ethics.** You tell the truth during an interview. Another candidate is willing to outright lie. Who all-too-often gets the job?
- **Inappropriate Interview Questions.** Did you give the "wrong answer"? Do you remember what you said when asked about age, ancestry, citizen-

ship, credit rating, criminal record, disabilities, family status, gender, military discharge, or religion?

CONTEXT OF THE HIGHER EDUCATION WORKPLACE

Perhaps the worse context issue occurs after you are hired on the tenure-track. It only takes a few months to realize you hate your colleagues, the dean, or maybe even the students. What now? You may be the product of a liberal arts education but did it really develop your skills to be a teacher? This is a no-win situation. If you fail in the academy, that's not good. It's even worse if you hate the job but are forced to keep it for thirty years.

CONCLUSION AND FALLACIES

The context of a situation plays a key role in shaping attitudes, behaviors, beliefs, and more. Understanding the context of a situation is the critical variable to fixing a subway system, responding to a crisis, seizing new opportunities in changing marketplaces, or evaluating a career in higher education. Hence:

Fallacy 14. The coverage of context is not an aspect of the liberal arts.

Reality 14. The liberal arts fail if they do not address an understanding of context by students, professors, and society.

Chapter Fifteen

Why Should Professors Encourage Pursuing Tipping Points and Sticky Messages? What's All the Commotion about Unstoppable Change?

> Nobody in Europe will be abandoned. Nobody in Europe will be excluded. Europe only succeeds if we work together.
>
> —Angela Merkel, chancellor of Germany

TIPPING POINTS

Malcolm Gladwell expands the concept of a tipping point as a moment in time when an unstoppable change (an epidemic) is about to occur. Such an event has:

- **Contagiousness.** Circumstances create a rapidly spreading influence that touches people and arouses them to action.
- **Impact.** Small changes have big effects on people, ideas, or communications, and can cause much disruption.
- **Speed.** Change happens in one dramatic moment. Although movement may start quietly, the impact is surprising and sudden. It's as though an underground earthquake in the middle of the ocean is largely unnoticed until it creates a tsunami that destroys a coastal area.

Three key factors create epidemics when we are making decisions.

- **Power of Context.** As already described, a major determinant of behavior.
- **Stickiness Factor.** A message makes a memorable impact. People remember and respond to it.

- **Law of the Few.** A tiny percentage of people build momentum. It can even be one person that determines the final outcome.

STICKINESS

Gladwell reminds us that our message must be "sticky" in someone's mind, be distinctive, and motivate a positive response. We find sticky messages everywhere, sculpted to produce a tipping point. Sticky ideas have six key attributes remembered by the acronym **SUCCESS**.

- **Stories.** Send a message in the form of a story.
- **Unexpectedness.** Start the story in a direction and change to a compelling outcome not foreseen in advance.
- **Concreteness.** Make sure the message has meaning.
- **Credibility.** Match the message to the belief system of the audience.
- **Emotions.** Frame the message so it is positive and pleasurable.
- **Sharp.** Make a compelling point.
- **Simplicity.** Design the message to be easy to grasp.

STICKY ADVERTISING MESSAGES

Advertising gives us sticky messages. How many can you identify?

- Nothing Outlasts the _________ Battery. It Keeps Going, and Going (1980s).
- With a Name like ________, It Has to be Good (1974).
- The Best Part of Waking up is ________ in Your Cup (1960s).
- A ____________ is Forever (1948).
- ____________, the Breakfast of Champions (1935).
- The Pause that Refreshes, ____________ (1929).
- ________________, Good to the Last Drop (1926).
- ________________, 99 and $^{44}/_{100}$ Percent Pure (1882).

The answers to the sticky advertising messages are below.

CONNECTIONS

Everybody is not created equal, and all things are not equally important. The key to sharing sticky messages is to recognize two types of connections.

- **Strong Connections.** We have these connections with our family, friends, co-workers, and neighbors. We see these people all the time.
- **Weak Connections.** These relationships are less frequent or even infrequent. They exist with associates at work, clerks in stores, classmates at school, and other casual acquaintances. We know things about these people but we do not know the people they know.

Among the few important people, Gladwell differentiates what they do into three categories.

- **Connectors.** Individuals with a special gift for bringing the world together.
- **Mavens.** Information specialists who pay close attention to details, possess considerable technical knowledge, and want to help others.
- **Salesmen.** Individuals with the skills to persuade skeptical people to join with or respond to the epidemic.

According to Gladwell, a tipping point occurs when we use our vast network of **weak connections**. Our strong connections occupy our world. They know what we know. Acquaintances occupy other worlds. They can be a source of social power. We rely on them for opportunities outside our vision.

ANSWERS TO STICKY ADVERTISING MESSAGES

- Nothing Outlasts the **Energizer** Battery. It Keeps Going, and Going (1980s).
- With a Name like **Smuckers**, It Has to be Good (1974).
- The Best Part of Waking up is **Folgers** in Your Cup (1960s).
- A **Diamond** is Forever (1948).
- **Wheaties**, the Breakfast of Champions (1935).
- The Pause that Refreshes, **Coca-Cola** (1929).
- **Maxwell House Coffee**, Good to the Last Drop (1926).
- **Ivory Soap**, 99 and $^{44}/_{100}$ Percent Pure (1882).

IKEA STICKY MESSAGES AND MORE

IKEA is the world's largest furniture retailer with 350 stores in forty-three countries. The Swedish firm is known for the modern architectural designs of its appliances and furniture. Its products offer an eco-friendly simplicity. Sticky messages are the name of the game, particularly contemporary design, low prices, wacky promotions, and customer enthusiasm.

QUESTION

IKEA offered a $4,000 gift certificate to the first person who arrived and smaller prizes to the next one hundred people in line at the opening of its Atlanta store in 2005. The message spread by word of mouth. How many hours early did the first person arrive? How many total people were present at opening time?

ANSWER

Roger Penguino, a twenty-four-year-old employee of Apple Computer, arrived seven days before the opening. More than two thousand people were present when the doors opened.

QUESTION

Comparing the Atlanta IKEA opening with the London opening a few months earlier, which was more successful?

ANSWER

This is the data. What do you think?

Factor	*Atlanta*	*London*
Time of opening	9:00 am	Midnight
Length of time opening	Twelve hours	Thirty minutes
Number of customers in line	Two thousand	Six thousand
Hospitalized	Zero	Six
Injured	Zero	Twenty-six

THREE WEAK CONNECTION STORIES

Professors can encourage students to employ word of mouth, law of the few, and weak connections to increase their chance to achieve personal goals. These are examples.

1. Alumni Connection

A woman decided to become active in the alumni association of her college. Even though she had graduated many years earlier, she had not stayed in touch with classmates or other alumni. Her motive was to seek help finding a new career opportunity.

She attended special events sponsored for alumni by the college. She arrived early, talked with strangers, made new friends, and engaged guest speakers. She described her activities, including the part about a career change. One of the alumni gave her a card and asked her to call his office. In a matter of weeks, she had an attractive job offer. It was at the company of the alumnus but not working with him. He opened the door to a sales representative position in a different department.

2. Job Search Connection

One of my students was looking for a new job when we discussed the law of the few. He had been searching for a while to no avail. After a class discussing weak connections, he sent a cover letter and resume to a network of acquaintances. Three weeks later, he got a call from the vice president of a major bank. He was invited to an interview and subsequently accepted an attractive position at the bank. After starting the job, he asked how the bank learned about him. It turns out that one of his acquaintances was the son of a senior executive in the bank. When the father mentioned to the son that the bank had an unexpected opening, the son gave his father the resume and a brief description of the man. One person started the movement that led to a phone call and a tipping point.

3. Promotion Connection

I have my own personal weak connection story. As a new faculty member, I was in a department with a talented female chairperson. She was asked by the academic vice president to accept a position as associate dean of the school. The discussion turned to her replacement. She told the vice president the names of the people in the department.

The vice president selected me to be the new chairperson. My qualifications? The only thing he knew was that I played basketball with him and other faculty and staff members at lunch.

SAINT PETER'S TIPPING POINT

A few years ago, Saint Peter's College had a struggling master's of business administration program. It required too many courses, included outdated topics, and used instructors who were out of touch with modern business. Gladwell's tipping point laid out the strategy to fix the system:

- **Change the Context.** Make the classroom more attractive. The college introduced a shorter curriculum, new courses, and brought in part-time faculty actively working in senior business positions.
- **Develop a Sticky Message.** The program was described and marketed in simple and compelling language.
- **Law of the Few.** Students and alumni were engaged to distribute the "sticky message" to local businesses and communities.

The classroom became attractive. The college had something to sell and even a stroke of good luck. A risk management concentration had been introduced in the program. The bankruptcy of Enron and new government requirements for accounting firms built interest in risk management. Enrollments soared.

SWEET BRIAR TIPPING POINT

Sweet Briar College is an all-women, liberal arts college in Virginia founded in 1901. For years, it experienced declining enrollments. In 2015, the college announced it would shut down at the end of the school year. One month later more than seven hundred alumni rallied with current students in support of continuing operations. A few alumni rallied many others who were weak connections and praised the context of the college with sticky messages about Sweet Briar's value.

QUESTION

What does Sweet Briar have to do with a tipping point?

ANSWER

Two things actually. The declining enrollment finally caused a tipping point with a sudden decision to close. The rally, begun by a few energized students and alumni and a sticky message about the history of the school, may have created a tipping point for sustained operation. Good things happened, and the college is working toward a tipping point. The story is continuing as this is being written.

CONCLUSION AND FALLACIES

A graduate's ability to think critically about the context of situations is a sticky message. This can lead college graduates to tipping points in their lives and careers. Hence:

Fallacy 15. A liberal arts education is lost in a time warp.
Reality 15. The liberal arts critically shape modern concepts such as tipping points and sticky messages.

Chapter Sixteen

How Should the Liberal Arts Handle Intuitive Thinking? When Do We Have Enough Information to Decide?

A good battle plan that you act on today can be better than a perfect one tomorrow.

—General George S. Patton, military leader

MV *BRAER*

In 1993, the MV *Braer*, an ocean-going ship, was carrying diesel oil in the dead of winter. It crashed upon rocks off the Shetland Islands near a small resort town with three hundred year-round residents and one forty-room hotel.

Within a single day, a crisis team arrived to contain the growing oil spill. Tugs from London and other ports would soon join the team with oil containment equipment. One hundred and fifty workers would work for three to four weeks to clean up the spill.

The crisis team leader needed sleeping accommodations for the workers. The hotel was closed tight for the winter. The owner refused to open it, explaining by telephone from London that he wanted it to be ready for the regular summer residents. Other facilities were not readily identifiable on the island. The team leader could set up tents or try to find other accommodations. He had thirty-six hours to find a solution.

QUESTION

What should the team leader do? If you ask the wrong question, you will always get the wrong answer. Instead we might ask, "What can he do?"

ANSWER

He bought the hotel. Think about what that involved.

- The owner demanded that he pay a higher price than the value of the hotel. Done!
- The owner would not sign over the deed until the money was in his bank account in London. That happened at the start of the next workday when modern technology allowed an instantaneous transfer of money.

QUESTION

The workers left after a month. What did Canadian Ultramar do with the hotel?

ANSWER

The company sold it back to the original owner. The loss was much less than the likely loss from indecision or inaction when cleaning up the spill.

SEQUENTIAL AND INTUITIVE REASONING

It may be argued that a liberal arts framework provides a solid understanding for logically resolving problems.

From the story of the MV *Braer*, we introduce Malcolm Gladwell's work highlighting decisions based on the amount of information.

- **"Thick Slice" or Sequential Reasoning.** Some decisions are made after collecting data, organizing it, and analyzing events and options.
- **"Thin Slice" or Intuition.** Other decisions are based on instinct or experience with no visible steps in the process.

Gladwell, in his book *Blink*, argued that thin slicing is often the best decision-making approach. Essentially, **"less is more."** The crisis team leader may have made a bad choice to buy the hotel, but wasting time to study alternatives could have been a disaster.

In making this judgment, let's acknowledge some caveats:

- **Recognizing Bias.** Prejudgments interfere with objective perspectives. Some people like something. Others dislike it. They make different decisions because they already formed beliefs or opinions on the matter.
- **Shaping Intuition.** People can learn how to improve the accuracy of their intuition. In many cases, a decision just "feels" right and it is.
- **Instinctive Error.** An intuitive decision can also be wrong. Do we have enough experience or knowledge to validate our belief?

CONFIDENCE ERROR

We want to feel confident that we are making the right decision. More evidence provides assurance, even as we select "facts" that support our decision. The pursuit of more information can run into problems with the help of our unconscious mind:

- **False Memories.** We claim to remember an event that we can prove never happened.
- **Distorted Memories.** We describe an event that did happen but our memory is confused or distorted.
- **Distorted Perceptions.** We can describe accurately a person, situation, or behavior with an interpretation that is not logical or realistic.

FALSE MEMORIES

A man and his wife were checking into a hotel on a crowded holiday weekend. The desk clerk said they had no reservation. The discussion became quite intense as they affirmed they left a written confirmation at home. The husband remembered specifically putting it in a travel folder in a file cabinet. The manager worked out the problem and the moment passed. When the couple returned home, the husband went to the cabinet with plans to email the confirmation. It was not there. Its existence was a false memory.

A colleague was teaching a business course. He used handouts of his own material. While discussing a topic with a class, he asked a question that received no student response. A little annoyed, he asked, "Why do you not read the material when I take the time to write it?" It turned out to be a distorted memory. He had not written it.

Gladwell reminds us that our instincts can be right or wrong. We must learn when to trust them. Snap judgments and first impressions can be educated and controlled.

DECISIONS UNDER PRESSURE OR IN DISPUTES

Gladwell presents dangers to thin slicing when we are making decisions in situations or stress. These lessons can help students develop better behaviors. Discussions can cover:

- **Criticism.** Negative statements find fault with the viewpoint or behavior of others.
- **Contempt.** An intense feeling that another person is inferior may be vocal, observable, or hidden.
- **Defensiveness.** A negative reaction to disagreement or criticism can display negative energy or anger.
- **Stonewalling.** A refusal to continue participation in a discussion can effectively destroy the ability to make any decision at all.

QUESTION

In a public meeting, two men are engaged in an intense vocal debate. One says, "Will you shut up and let me finish?" What is the likely reaction of the other individual?

ANSWER

Not good. He might respond, "Sorry. Go ahead." He is probably thinking, "To hell with you. When I speak, you will be my target."

QUESTION

A husband and wife are engaged in an intense argument. The wife says, "Will you shut up and let me finish?" The husband says nothing. What is he thinking?

ANSWER

He could be thinking, "You are so miserable. You remind me of your mother."

The lesson here is simple. When using thin slicing, we need to help others beware of subconscious factors that can destroy the benefits of good intuitive decision making.

QUESTION

In the United States, many Democrats and Republicans do not like each other because they make thin slice decisions that are wrong. Do you agree?

ANSWER

Which of the following "thin slices" do you prefer?

- Republicans can have contempt for Democrats who believe in "socialism," advocate gay marriage, and want the government to take money from hard-working families to give to the sick, lame, and lazy.
- Democrats can dislike Republicans who support unrestrained and unethical capitalism, advocate religion trumping science, and deny decent health care to those who are less fortunate.

QUESTION

Students tend to enjoy discussions about gender differences if kept in check by the professor. As an example, it appears likely that men and women can be stereotyped by the way they show contempt publicly. What is the difference?

ANSWER

Class discussions tend to support the following:

- **Men.** They stonewall by withdrawing from discussion and displaying silent irritation. The other party is not worth the time or energy to have a discussion.
- **Women.** They criticize by intensifying the situation and demanding answers to their questions. The other party has no value but should be told the errors of thinking that are being made.

IMPULSE AND DELIBERATE DECISIONS

Considerable research has been focused on decisions by two categories of people:

- **Impulse Deciders.** They do little research or prior hunting for evidence. They decide and move on.
- **Deliberate Deciders.** They conduct detailed prior investigation. They hesitate before deciding.

QUESTION

Gladwell describes researchers who identified people as impulse and deliberate buyers in two stores:

- **Department Store.** These buyers purchased relatively simple items.
- **IKEA.** These buyers purchased furniture.

After the passage of several weeks, the researchers contacted the buyers. Which group was happier with its purchases?

ANSWER

With the relatively simple purchases, the deliberate buyers were happier. With the more complex furniture purchases, impulse buyers were happier.

Lesson Learned: Less may not always be more. On straightforward choices, the experiments showed that deliberate analysis is best. In situations where many variables must be juggled, our intuition may do a better job. Less is more (thin slice) in complex situations.

FREUD ON THIN SLICES

Lest we think that thick and thin slices are a revolutionary decision-making concept, Gladwell suggests we consider the words of Sigmund Freud (1856–1939):

> When making a decision of minor importance, I have always found it advantageous to consider all the pros and cons. In vital matters, however, such as the choice of a mate or a profession, the decision should come from the un-

conscious, from somewhere inside ourselves. (Quote taken from http://www.goodreads.com/quotes/94440-when-making-a-decision-of-minor-importance-i-have-always)

PREFERENCE FOR THIN SLICES?

Despite the available research on intuition in decision making, many people prefer quantitative methods and formal models as superior tools for decision making. Why does this happen?

ANSWER

Sequential reasoning can be taught. Revenues minus expenses calculates a profit. How to build a house can be learned by an apprentice using a step-by-step checklist. Intuition cannot be taught. It can be honed by the liberal arts and enhanced by experiences that reveal what works and what fails.

QUESTION

If we move quickly, we can make a good decision today. If we take time to investigate the details, we may be able to make a better decision in a month. What should we do?

ANSWER

This decision reflects both circumstances and personal style. Some opportunities are fleeting, whereas other situations are a crisis. Some people need only a bit of information to start moving, whereas others need a detailed understanding of data and options.

QUESTION

Which of the following tells us the most about someone? Is it a person's clothing, hobby, office or cubicle, automobile, medicine cabinet, or participation as a student in class?

ANSWER

All of them are thin slices of information to reach conclusions about others.

QUESTION

A company has job descriptions for all employees. It advertises nationally, screens dozens of resumes, and interviews ten to fifteen finalists. Another company asks managers to attend professional conferences. It tells them to talk with colleagues in other organizations and invite some of them to discuss joining the company. Which approach will produce a more skilled workforce?

ANSWER

We have considerable evidence that "less is more" when making hiring decisions.

THIN SLICE STRATEGIES AND SITUATIONS

Thick and thin slice behavior links to thinking and decision making:

- **Strategic Decisions.** We display strategic skills when we identify risk or opportunity and make correct decisions to respond.
- **Situational Adjustments.** Behaviors need to change when conditions do not match our plans.

CONCLUSION AND FALLACIES

The lesson of "less is more" is that decision making, though always a process, should be based upon the balance of sequential and intuitive reasoning. A thick slice can be powerful if conditions allow the time to collect and analyze data. A thin slice wins when time is of the essence. Bringing the two approaches together seems to make the most sense. Hence:

Fallacy 16. Liberal arts bog students down with evidence before deciding.
Reality 16. Liberal arts recognize the validity of intuitive approaches to decision making.

Chapter Seventeen

How Should the Liberal Arts Handle Disruptive Innovation? Will We Break if We Don't Prepare to Bend?

> The ultimate measure of a man is not where he stands in moments of comfort and convenience, but where he stands at times of challenge and controversy.
>
> —Martin Luther King Jr., American clergyman and political activist

TOO GOOD TO BE TRUE

"If you are paying more than three-quarters of a percent for your mortgage, call xxx-508-2300 now and refinance your home." I can still hear the radio commercials that began in 2004 as I drove home from work. I am reminded of the day when my administrative assistant told me, "My son got a mortgage. Nothing down. He will pay only interest for the first two years. I told him no one would give you a mortgage. His reply was that I was out of touch. I did not know how things worked."

When did mortgage terms become so ridiculously lax? What scam was underway? Who would fall for such a commercial? Something was wrong. It was demonstrated a few years later when the man could not make his loan payments and the bank foreclosed on his home.

QUESTION

Why does the liberal arts examine concepts broadly in literature, history, politics, and mathematics when these areas have little immediate impact on our lives?

ANSWER

Ah, but they do as they prepare us for disruptive change. In 1905, George Santayana wrote "Those who cannot remember the past are condemned to repeat it." Perhaps the young man took out a mortgage he could not afford because he never heard of the past economic bubbles.

- **The Dutch Tulip Bubble.** All right. We do not expect people to remember "Tulipmania" in Holland in the 1630s. Tulip prices soared twenty-fold before plunging 99 percent. Some bulbs commanded prices greater than the prices of luxury homes.
- **The Dot-Com Bubble.** We might expect people to remember a bubble in high-tech stock prices in the late 1990s. Hundreds of dot-com companies achieved multibillion dollar valuations as soon as they went public. One stock index went from five hundred to five thousand before crashing back to one thousand.

DISRUPTIVE INNOVATION

The liberal arts try to prepare us for disruptive innovation, a dramatic change in our lives that displaces our established behaviors. The Internet and cell phones are examples.

QUESTION

In the twentieth century, the automobile displaced the horse-drawn vehicle as a method of transportation. Was the automobile a disruptive innovation?

ANSWER

No. The automobile itself was a sustaining innovation. It improved the speed of travel for wealthy members of society in local areas where roads were adequately maintained. After the invention of the automobile, cars shared the roads with horses and buggies.

QUESTION

Did the automobile contribute to a disruptive innovation?

ANSWER

Most definitely. The disruptive innovation was that workers with more time and money could afford lower-cost cars to drive on new roads. It was caused by a combination of factors:

- **Assembly Line.** Henry Ford created a process to build low-cost vehicles.
- **Rising Income Levels.** Ford and others had efficient operations that allowed them to raise the income level for workers.
- **Shorter Work Week and Work Day.** Ford and others also could afford to shorten the time workers spent on the job giving them time to drive cars.

The rest was history.

BLACK SWAN

The vocabulary of disruption was expanded when Nassim Taleb coined the term "black swan" to describe an unforeseen event with three characteristics.

- **Rare Event.** The possibility of an incident that lies outside our normal expectations.
- **Extreme Consequence.** The incident poses a grave threat or challenge to our activities and us.
- **Surprise.** We do not see it in advance. It comes upon us unexpectedly and we do not immediately understand what happened.

QUESTION

Why did Taleb select the terminology "black swan"?

ANSWER

He got it from an early belief of Europeans and others that all swans were white. The discovery of Australia by James Cook in 1770 brought the news that the continent had black swans.

QUESTION

On the last Thursday in November, a black swan event occurs every year in the United States. What is the event and for whom is it a black swan?

ANSWER

The event is Thanksgiving. For a turkey, which has been pampered and fed generously for all its life, Thanksgiving is a black swan.

LIBERAL ARTS TREATMENT OF U.S. HOUSING CRISIS

The young man who made a bad choice on a mortgage was not alone. Forgetting the lessons of bubbles, Americans switched into real estate in a mistaken belief that it was a safe investment. Prices nearly doubled from 2002 to 2006 despite clear signs of an unsustainable frenzy.

How should we tell the story of the crisis in a history, economics, or political science course? A lecture on its statistics will soon be forgotten. How about re-creating the situation at a moment in time?

The year is 2005. We are in the office of a local savings bank. Our young man is talking to a loan officer.

WELCOME

Applicant: I would like to buy a house but I don't have a down payment.

Loan Officer: No problem. I have access to five hundred banks. I can get you a loan.

Applicant: What size loan?

Loan Officer: You are purchasing a $450,000 house. Don't worry that it was $400,000 last week. The seller agreed to make a $50,000 down payment.

Applicant: Excellent.

MONTHLY PAYMENT

Loan Officer: Here is your payment.

Applicant: Wow. I am not sure I can handle that.

Loan Officer: Here is your payment if we charge interest only for three years at 3 percent. Then, the rate will adjust to 7 percent and you can reduce the principal.

Applicant: Perfect. I can handle that.

ABILITY TO PAY

Loan Officer: I need to know your annual earnings from your job.

Applicant: If I get a promotion, $45,000.

Loan Officer: Are you sure it will not be more? What is the most it could be?

Applicant: With two promotions, $90,000.

Loan Officer: Ninety thousand dollars it is. You look like an honest person.

Applicant: I am.

LOAN APPROVAL

Loan Officer: Good news. We got a loan for $400,000 with interest-only payments at 3 percent for three years and an attractive 8 percent rate for twenty-seven more years.

Applicant: I thought the long-term rate would be 7 percent.

Loan Officer: I could not get it. Eight percent is a good deal.

Applicant: What happens if I cannot make the payments at the end of three years?

Loan Officer: No problem. You see home prices. Sell the house at a profit and buy another house.

Applicant: Only in America!

The mortgage house of cards collapsed in 2008 when millions of homeowners failed to make their mortgage payments and lost their homes. The defaults led to a near disaster for the international financial community.

QUESTION

Was the 2008 financial crisis a disruptive innovation or a legitimate black swan?

ANSWER

Some people saw it. In 2003, Warren Buffett, arguably the best investor of his time, wrote the following five years before the crisis:

> Charlie Munger [Buffett's partner at Berkshire Hathaway] and I are of one mind in how we feel about derivatives and the trading activities that go with them. . . .
>
> We try to be alert to any sort of mega-catastrophe risk, and that posture may make us unduly apprehensive about the burgeoning quantities of long-term derivatives contracts and the massive amount of uncollateralized receivables that is growing alongside. . . .
>
> In our view, however, derivatives are **financial weapons of mass destruction**, carrying dangers that, while now latent, are potentially lethal. (Warren Buffett, "Letter to Shareholders of Berkshire Hathaway," 2002)

QUESTION

Is Warrant Buffett the product of the liberal arts?

ANSWER

He was exposed to a liberal arts foundation as a business administration undergraduate at the University of Pennsylvania and University of Nebraska. His master's degree from Columbia University also likely shaped his keen vision.

QUESTION

Most people recognize that prevention is better than recovery when it comes to negative disruption. Does Taleb believe we can reward prevention?

ANSWER

Not really. A legislator who advocated bulletproof, locked cockpit doors prior to 9/11 would die unknown, not to mention being despised by airlines.

LESSON LEARNED

Disruptive innovation ties together important concepts needed to make effective decisions. We do not always make steady progress toward our goals. Instead, success may result from major changes that require totally new ways of thinking.

CONCLUSION AND FALLACIES

Disruption may or may not be welcome but creatively responding to it is critical. Disruptive innovation is needed to prosper. Hence:

Fallacy 17. Liberal arts encourage stability in decision making.
Reality 17. Liberal arts help develop skills to deal with disruptive innovation.

Part V

REACHING BEYOND THE CLASSROOM

Chapter Eighteen

Why Should Professors Help Students Understand Risk, Uncertainty, and Opportunity? What's All This Talk about the Future?

Failure is simply an opportunity to begin again, this time more intelligently.

—Henry Ford, American industrialist

RISK AND UNCERTAINTY

A critical mark of an educated person is an understanding how to deal with risk and uncertainty. Definitions:

- **Risk.** The possibility that something will go wrong and thus cause harm to people, assets, or anything of value.
- **Uncertainty.** A situation or condition not predictable in advance as to what will happen, when it will happen, or how much impact it will have.

QUESTION

A stranger asks if you want to buy his car for the Blue Book value. He refuses to allow you to take a test drive. Would you buy the car?

ANSWER

You should not buy the car. Uncertainty trumps risk. The seller knows more than you. Even with a discount from the Blue Book value, you cannot determine a fair price without more information.

QUESTION

The stranger tells you that your good friend will vouch for him. The friend is trustworthy and reliable. Would you reconsider buying the car?

ANSWER

Of course. But the risk is still largely unknown due to other factors. Rating agencies vouched for toxic assets in the 2008 financial crisis. If the friend does not know the individual is a crook, the testimony of honesty is worthless.

QUESTION

A man has made twenty-five thousand automobile trips as a driver in the past ten years. He never drank alcohol before driving and he never had an accident. Tonight, he is leaving an office party after a stressful two weeks of work. He has been drinking moderately. What are the odds of having an accident while driving based on the past statistics?

ANSWER

Who knows? The past statistics for the number of instances driving while stressed and intoxicated is zero.

QUESTION

An exposure is a condition where risk could cause a loss. A peril is the immediate cause of a loss. A hazard is a behavior that increases the possibility or severity of a loss. A family purchases a dog. With respect to the possibility of your dog being kidnapped by a stranger, what is an exposure, a peril, and a hazard?

ANSWER

The exposure is simply owning the dog. The kidnapping is a peril. It would be a hazard to allow the dog to go outside without an adult watching it.

QUESTION

What is the difference between kidnapping and anything else than can cause the loss of a dog?

ANSWER

Kidnapping is a risk the moment we recognize it. We can conceive of it and take steps to manage it. Many other things are uncertainties. As an example, we would not be prepared for the dog to catch a disease that is unknown to modern veterinarians.

HURRICANE IRENE

In 2011, Hurricane Irene hit the state of New Jersey as a category three storm. New Jersey Transit operates a commuter train system. Its extensive network employs many trains that use electricity for power.

With advance notice of the impending storm, New Jersey Transit carefully moved its trains from vulnerable positions to a location near the border of the state of Pennsylvania, ninety miles away. Once the storm was over, the trains could quickly be brought back into service. Unfortunately, Irene damaged electrical power lines and the trains were stalled for many days until lines were restored.

HURRICANE SANDY

In 2012, another storm threatened. New Jersey Transit remembered the lessons from Hurricane Irene. This time the trains were placed in a low-lying area near the Hudson River and Newark Bay. A ten-meter high storm surge hit the area flooding eighty-four multilevel brand new passenger cars and five locomotives. The damage exceeded $120 million.

A different story occurred in New York City's subways. The Metropolitan Transit Authority (MTA) moved its trains out of flood-prone areas and removed the electrical signals from its tunnels. When water streamed through the streets of lower Manhattan and poured into subway entrances, it did minimal damage to equipment. Yes, the tunnels flooded but subway workers quickly pumped out the water and replaced the electric signals. Very quickly, subway service was restored.

Other success and failure stories occurred. Goldman Sachs, for example, had "a massive wall of sandbags" outside the front entrance to its office in the flooded areas of lower Manhattan and Jersey City. The bank thus avoided major damage to the facilities. Goldman employees worked from home for a few days before reopening their offices with the help of portable generators. This compares to the nearby Verizon headquarters where a switching center in the basement flooded causing extensive damage.

UNCERTAINTY WITH TROPICAL CYCLONES

The back-to-back hurricanes Irene and Sandy show us the role of uncertainty, even in situations where we have risk management. One of the stories is particularly poignant. The MTA invited workers to stay on the job and get paid for ninety-six hours of work in four consecutive days when they would be on call twenty-four hours a day.

QUESTION

We can describe the hurricane stories to a liberal arts honors class. Then, we can ask them why the MTA would pay workers to sit and wait. Would they have answers?

ANSWER

They would point out that the available manpower allowed the MTA to respond to changing conditions. A plan was in place to address either risk or uncertainty. It gave priority to bring back essential activities in the short-term.

QUESTION

Gas stations had plenty of notice about the approach of Hurricane Sandy. Most wanted to open the next day. Were they ready?

ANSWER

Some were. They stockpiled gasoline in their stations and others placed orders for gas from refineries immediately after the storm. It was good risk management but not so good on uncertainty. Some stations did not stock up so they had no gasoline when the refineries lost their electricity and could not produce it. Many lost electricity and had no backup generators to pump the gasoline. If they had local generators and gasoline, many customers could not make purchases. Customers typically paid with credit cards, and the links to credit card companies were not working because of the absence of electricity. In some areas, it took two weeks to fully restore electricity and normal gasoline operations.

UNCERTAINTY IN MEDIOCRISTAN AND EXTREMISTAN

Understanding risk and uncertainty links to earlier discussions. Can we predict the severity of risk? It is easier in Mediocristan than in Extremistan.

QUESTION

A weight loss program with one thousand people measured an average weight loss of twenty-four pounds with a diet plan. To show greater success, the sponsors added five individuals whose weight loss averaged one hundred pounds. Did our results change dramatically?

ANSWER

This is Mediocristan. When they shared their findings, the results showed little variation.

- **Original.** Twenty-five thousand pounds were lost.
- **Revised.** 25,500 pounds were lost.
- **Original.** Average loss was twenty-five pounds (25,000/1,000).
- **Revised.** Average loss was 25.4 pounds (25,500/1,005).

UNCERTAINTY IN EXTREMISTAN

A survey of one thousand people determined that the average annual income was $25,000. Seeking to show a higher standard of living, the sponsors added an individual who earned a bonus of $10 million. The results were extreme.

- **Original.** Twenty-five million dollars was total income.
- **Revised.** Thirty-five million dollars was total income.
- **Original.** Average income was $25,000 ($25,000,000/1,000).
- **Revised.** Average income was $34,960 ($35,000,000/1,001).

There are two lessons learned from the weight loss and annual income comparisons:

- **Mediocristan.** When facing uncertainty in this world, an exception to the expectation has little impact.
- **Extremistan.** When facing uncertainty here, an exception to the expectation has large impact.

QUESTION

When the financial crisis occurred in September 2007, a university wanted to know the impact on its enrollments for the 2008 spring term. The request was for the most likely, best, and worst possibilities. Is this a sound request?

ANSWER

It depends on where the crisis put the university. Forecasting enrollment in the normal course of business is Mediocristan. The financial crisis enrollment predictions deal with an uncertainty, not a risk. In the new Extremistan, the forecasts became:

- **Most Likely.** The prior forecast based on historical data was no longer likely.
- **Best Case.** No information existed on what would be best under unknown circumstances.
- **Worst Case.** Bankruptcy if the whole system collapsed.

HEDGEHOG AND FOX PROFILE

Isaiah Berlin, a social and political philosopher, made a distinction between two types of people who face uncertainty. As subsequently reported by Nate Silver, an American statistician and writer (*The Signal and the Noise*, Penguin Books, 2012), they are:

- **Hedgehog.** An individual who knows "one big thing." This person usually does not change his mind nor does he acknowledge mistakes. He abides by orderly processes and firmly believes he is always right when making decisions.
- **Fox.** This person knows many things as he borrows ideas from many areas. He pursues knowledge and acknowledges his mistakes. He knows the world is complex and thus is cautious when making a decision.

QUESTION

Of the hedgehog and the fox, which person does a better job of dealing with uncertainty?

ANSWER

Without doubt, it is the fox. The only way we prepare for the unknown is to recognize that we are often wrong when we forecast and we must constantly seek new information. The hedgehog living in an orderly world where we know almost everything is not prepared to be resilient in the face of the unexpected.

NIGERIAN KIDNAPPING

A sizable exposure is posed by kidnapping all over the world. One story comes from Nigeria where kidnapping foreign executives is big business, as much as $100 million a year.

It can be exciting. Imagine the scene outside Goodfellas, a popular and usually crowded bar in Port Harcourt. Music is playing. Beer is flowing. Two cars pull up. Men wearing ski masks jump out and burst into the bar pointing automatic rifles and shouting for everyone to lie on the floor. They select individuals who appear to be most valuable and take them away.

On one occasion, a selected victim was John, a friendly Scotsman working for a foreign oil company. He was driven to the waterfront, loaded into a speedboat, and taken to an island in the Nigerian delta.

His company was contacted to pay a ransom. While negotiations took place, the situation was not unpleasant in the hostage camp. The militants built a makeshift hut for John and his fellow hostages while singing Christian hymns and drinking a locally made liquor. Helicopters passed over the camp occasionally, though no one ever seriously thought about trying to escape. They would be lost without GPS devices, maps, or compasses.

After ten days, John was given fresh clothes, taken to a sandy beach, and released. The *New York Times* reporter who told the story was in Port Harcourt. On his last night, he had dinner at Cheers Bar with a kidnapper who asked to be identified by his nom de guerre, De Don.

Three years earlier, De Don graduated from a university with a degree in political science. While there, he joined a campus gang known as the Greenlanders. When he could not find work after graduation, he tapped into the Greenlanders alumni network and asked for help. Soon he was living in the Delta as part of a kidnapping syndicate. He made enough money to rent an apartment and buy a used Mercedes. He also supported his family and opened a beauty salon for one of his girlfriends.

QUESTION

Is the threat of kidnapping in Nigeria a risk or uncertainty?

ANSWER

Clearly an uncertainty that can happen at any time. Also, a risk as it can be managed by efforts to avoid public places.

PICK THE WINNER OF THE KENTUCKY DERBY

This story starts with a class that was making a point about overconfidence. Students were given information about horses that were the ten top finishers in a Kentucky Derby race. With each horse was information on its prior racing record and an evaluation by a handicapping expert. Students were asked to forecast the first place, second place, and third place finishers and provide an estimate of their confidence that they picked the winners.

The experiment has been conducted multiple times. The outcome was always the same. Few people picked more than one of the top three horses. Rarely did someone pick the actual winner. Most submissions showed high confidence in totally wrong guesses.

The goal was to teach students to be careful of overconfidence. That was not the outcome. Instead, they learned about something else.

- When students picked horses with the lowest odds and lost, they did not feel the loss. If the horse had won, a return of three dollars on a two dollar bet was trivial.
- On the other hand, betting on a horse with high odds would produce fewer wins but a single success would be exciting. Such a bet would not be irrational at all.

QUESTION

The exercise caused one student to use a handheld device to look up the highest odds on a winning horse in Kentucky Derby history. Do long shots ever win?

ANSWER

Sent off at odds of ninety-two to one, Donerail paid $184 to win in 1913. This discovery raised the excitement level in the whole class even though it had nothing to do with the exercise. Students learned that winning a gamble produces more than a statistical success. It excites the emotions with a feeling that we are winners. A student once observed, "My dad went to the track all the time. I don't know how he did except once. He bet on a thirty to one long shot that won the race. I can hear him now. 'I won three hundred dollars at the racetrack on a two-dollar bet.'"

QUESTION

What was the lesson learned from the Kentucky Derby race story?

ANSWER

It was partly the danger of overconfidence but it also provided an insight into risk and uncertainty. A small gamble involves little loss but also not much return. If we are going to have a big win in life, we occasionally might have to take a big gamble.

CONCLUSION AND FALLACIES

A significant challenge for the liberal arts is to prepare students to seize opportunity. In their personal lives and careers, they must recognize the risks that can be managed and the uncertainty that can upset the "best-laid plans of mice and men." Also, they need to assess taking a chance to achieve something out of the ordinary. Hence:

Fallacy 18. Liberal arts encourage students to resist taking chances.
Reality 18. The liberal arts shape an understanding of risk and uncertainly needed by students, employers, and society.

Chapter Nineteen

Do Professors Know What They Think They Know? What is the Danger of Too Much Confidence?

We tried very hard not to be overconfident, because when you get overconfident, that's when something snaps up and bites you.

—Neil Armstrong, American astronaut and the first person to walk on the moon

CONFIDENCE IN THE LIBERAL ARTS

It is only a short step from overconfidence to making bad decisions on why things happen and what will happen in the future. The liberal arts help us understand what we know and don't know. Building on the work of Nassim Taleb, let's examine this issue.

QUESTION

In 1981, Yale professor and Nobel Prize winner Robert Shiller demonstrated that stock markets are irrational. Robert Merton, Nobel Prize winner and professor at the Massachusetts Institute of Technology, disagreed, saying markets are efficient and investors could not take advantage of inefficiencies. He won the Nobel Prize in 1997. Who was right?

ANSWER

Shiller was right. In 1994, Merton became a founder of a hedge fund designed to take advantage of market inefficiencies. It used complex statistics and earned 40 percent a year until 1997. The Russian and Asian financial crises in 1998 caused it to lose $5 billion. It closed in 2000.

Epilogue. Merton did not return his Nobel Prize in Economics.

QUESTION

Professor Alan Sok submitted a paper in 1996 to a scholarly journal published by Duke University Press. The title was "Transgressing the Boundaries: Towards a Transformative Hermeneutics of Quantum Gravity." What impact did this single paper have on modern science?

ANSWER

It had no impact. Sokal subsequently announced that his paper was outright nonsense presenting silly quotations about mathematics and physics.

QUESTION

In 1938, British Prime Minister Neville Chamberlain met with Adolf Hitler in Munich and returned to Great Britain with the proclamation:

> My good friends . . . there has come back from Germany to Downing Street . . . peace with honor. I believe it is peace for our time.

Was he right?

ANSWER

Not exactly. A year later, Great Britain was at war with Germany. It was in all the papers.

KNOWLEDGE AND EXPERTISE

Professors often think they are experts when they really aren't. They are confident in situations where no evidence supports their beliefs. They have limited facts and assume what they do not know. They defend what is not easily supported by logic or knowledge.

Why does this happen? Many reasons, including a failure to distinguish the difference between science and art:

- **Science.** A body of knowledge that reveals nature and basic principles. We make them into a discipline or field of study.
- **Art.** An applied skill that makes something happen. It is shaped by beliefs, goals, and situations.

QUESTION

Is decision making an art or a science?

ANSWER

It can be either or both depending upon the evidence available and the outcome of past data. The possibilities are:

- **Evidence Based.** Data provides the necessary knowledge resembling a science. Take an aspirin for a headache because past practice shows it reduces pain.
- **Opinion Based.** Where no data is reliable, everybody can have a different view. Some people like a painting and some don't.
- **Mixed Criteria.** When we have data and preferences, a balanced approach is recommended. Does the aspiring professor want a PhD from Ohio State or Rutgers? Compare academic criteria plus student preferences for non-academic factors.

QUESTION

What is an expert in the academy?

ANSWER

A cynic might say, "Any professor in his own mind." The dictionary would say a person with extensive knowledge based on research in a particular area of study and who is supported by a credentials, practice, publications, or experience.

QUESTION

How does a professor demonstrate expertise?

ANSWER

Initially by obtaining a doctorate and writing a dissertation.

QUESTION

Does the expertise of a professor differ from that of a doctor or lawyer?

ANSWER

Yes indeed. The professor takes expertise and uses it in a narrow effort to help students learn and personally obtain approval for tenure. Doctors and lawyers are not recognized for their expertise until they broaden their knowledge with experience applying it.

QUESTION

Are professors, doctors, and lawyers similar in any ways with respect to expertise?

ANSWER

Yes. In addition to initial credentials, they have tendencies toward overconfidence. When they are right, they believe it is the result of depth of understanding. When wrong, they blame events that are random or outside their control.

QUESTION

What about evidence that conflicts with their beliefs?

ANSWER

It is often ignored. Do they know what they know? Not really. They know what they believe and that leads to excess confidence, a situation that heightens when they are under pressure. A poor rating from students, loss of a lawsuit, or death on an operating table come to mind.

MISLEADING AND MEANINGLESS INFORMATION

Another source of overconfidence comes from the fact that many beliefs about conventional knowledge are wrong or worthless. Academic discussions lead institutions and their graduates in wrong directions. We lock down on assumptions or opinions that serve our own needs and lose all intellectual rigor as we argue our positions.

QUESTION

Say the name of your favorite college or university and then combine it with one of the following phrases. What did you say about the character or value of the school?

- The Place to Be!
- Start Here, Go Anywhere.
- A Tradition of Leadership.
- Education One Student at a Time.
- Where You're a Name, Not a Number.
- Our Purpose is to Make Minds, not Careers.

ANSWER

Nothing really. Do you think?

IMAGINATION

Another factor in overconfidence occurs from information that can frighten or excite us. Our perception of events arises from a single murder in the park, accident on a motorcycle, or the wrong medication causing death in a hospital.

The more we can imagine something sensational, the greater the emotional reaction. This can make or destroy our confidence without any other factor involved.

SILENT EVIDENCE

Nassim Taleb describes our tendency to filter our information that doesn't fit our beliefs. Silent evidence is that which is ignored. A serious weakness in thinking occurs from this behavior.

- **Unknown Silent Evidence.** The evening news showed ten survivors of a plane crash where seventy people lost their lives. As the plane was dropping, they joined together in prayer. Did the prayer save their lives? The obvious question. Did any of the dead also pray?
- **Known Silent Evidence.** A drug saves ten thousand people a year but side effects kill ten others. Will a doctor prescribe it? Products and services are banned all the time when risks are statistically insignificant.

Taleb was annoyed by one example of silent evidence. His book *The Black Swan* sold 1.5 million copies, was translated into twenty-seven languages, and spent seventeen weeks on the *New York Time*s bestseller list. After the publication, an editor was asked to explain the success. He said the book was successful partly or largely because it had an animal and color on the cover.

QUESTION

Our theories often come from generalizing silent evidence. With respect to book sales, we can theorize success comes from writing a good book. Does this work?

ANSWER

Maybe yes and maybe no. More than 90 percent of U.S. published books fail to achieve sales success. A better approach is to promote the book on a popular television show or find a way to attract attention with social media.

LIBERAL ARTS AND OVERCONFIDENCE

If we want to help college students improve their awareness of overconfidence, we can test them.

QUESTION

A man was on trial for murdering his wife. The prosecution introduced evidence that the man was an inveterate wife abuser. The defendant's lawyer introduced statistics that male partners batter four million women every year. At the same time, her partner ultimately murders only one in twenty-five hundred. Does this evidence make us confident that the man did not commit the murder?

ANSWER

The answer is no. The statistic was introduced at the O. J. Simpson trial. However, Nicole Brown Simpson was already dead. The relevant question is, "What percent of battered women are killed by their abusers?" The answer was 90 percent, but it did not come up in the trial. Leonard Mlodinow cites this story in *The Drunkard's Walk: How Randomness Rules our Lives.*

WILL ROGERS ON AVOIDING EXCESS CONFIDENCE

Some of the best suggestions for combatting overconfidence come from the American philosopher Will Rogers. He was a humorist who brought a quiet wisdom to decision making. Answer the questions, then check your answers.

1. What did Will Rogers say about the spurs on the boots of a cowboy?
2. What did Will Rogers say about good judgment, bad judgment, and experience?
3. What did Will Rogers say about letting the cat out of the bag?
4. What did Will Rogers say about riding ahead of the herd?
5. What did Will Rogers say about the right strategy when you find yourself in a hole?
6. What did Will Rogers say about the quickest way to double your money?
7. What did Will Rogers say about shutting up?

The answers are below.

CONCLUSION AND FALLACIES

If we agree that excess confidence can be dangerous, the liberal arts can spread the message to others. One way to do it is to demonstrate the tendency to ignore or fail to seek new information when we lack information but need to adjust our behavior by seeking feedback. This is one of the most important takeaways from a liberal arts education. Maybe we are not doing such a good job because so many college graduates do not seem to know the lesson. Hence:

Fallacy 19. The academy builds student confidence in decision making.
Reality 19. The academy needs to alert students to the danger of overconfidence when they lack the information needed to make good decisions.

ANSWERS TO WISDOM OF WILL ROGERS.

1. Don't squat with your spurs on.
2. Good judgment comes from experience, and a lot of that comes from bad judgment.
3. Lettin' the cat outta the bag is a whole lot easier 'n puttin' it back in.
4. If you're ridin' ahead of the herd, take a look back every now and then to make sure it's still there.
5. If you find yourself in a hole, the first thing to do is stop digging.
6. The quickest way to double your money is to fold it over and put it back in your pocket.
7. Never miss a good chance to shut up.

Chapter Twenty

Is Collaboration the Hallmark of a Liberal Arts Education? Can People See Further if They Stand on the Shoulders of Others?

Alone we can do so little; together we can do so much.

—Helen Keller, American author and political activist

COLLABORATION

Collaboration occurs when two or more people work together to achieve a common goal. A joint effort increases available knowledge, shares it, creates learning from new viewpoints, and seeks to develop a consensus. People working together are more likely to find solutions to problems.

QUESTION

Dr. Eboo Patel, the founder of Interfaith Cooperation, argues that an interactive seminar discussing Plato's relevance to contemporary situations is a better preparation for the jobs of the future. Is he right?

ANSWER

Could be. He points out that such collaboration requires you to master knowledge, listen carefully to diverse points of view, communicate your own viewpoint, accept disappointment, and rebound with a stronger argument. This collaboration in the space of a few minutes in an actual room with actual people is the essence of learning.

QUESTION

What does Dr. Patel call this process of collaboration?

ANSWER

Simply, it is the "hallmark of a liberal education."

QUESTION

Does collaboration require leadership or management?

ANSWER

It requires management, not necessarily leadership. Results come from open access, decentralization, and equality among contributors.

QUESTION

Versatility describes a range of behaviors. Does high versatility enhance collaboration?

ANSWER

Yes. If individuals are open to new behaviors, they are also open to new ideas. High versatility allows creativity to overcome consistency.

QUESTION

What else enhances collaboration?

ANSWER

The presence of people with high emotional intelligence.

QUESTION

What about the accuracy of collaborative efforts? People say things that are not supported by evidence. Statements, representations, and misconceptions become a problem. Do we need to be concerned about the accuracy in collaboration?

ANSWER

Not really. *Nature* magazine compared *Wikipedia* and the *Encyclopedia Britannica*. The two sources were quite close in terms of errors. Graduate students at Nottingham University examined *Wikipedia* articles. Only a small percentage of students found errors. They ranked the articles as credible.

GOLDCORP

The following story shows an unusual collaboration to achieve a surprise solution to a problem. It was first told in *Wikinomics*, a book by Don Tapscott and Anthony Williams.

The story deals with GoldCorp, a company with gold mining operations in Ontario, Canada. It was concerned that its underground gold was being depleted and the company's geologists were not successful in finding new deposits.

At a conference at the Massachusetts Institute of Technology in 1999, Rob McEwen, chief executive officer of GoldCorp, learned about the Linux personal computer operating system. Linus Torvalds shared the code with thousands of anonymous programmers who then created thousands of new applications.

McEwen returned home and released to the Internet all the company's geologic data from 1948 to 1999. He invited geologists to find new deposits of gold in the GoldCorp Challenge in March 2000. The company offered prizes of more than a half-million dollars for the best estimates of the location of gold deposits. More than one thousand individuals tackled four hundred megabytes of data.

QUESTION

What do you think were the results of the collaborative effort of one thousand strangers?

ANSWER

The results were striking. Entries identified 110 potential large deposits, half of which had never been previously identified. McEwen ordered $10 million to be spent drilling in the deepest and remotest areas of the mine. The company discovered rich new gold deposits in 80 of the 110 locations. The company grew in revenues from $100 million to $9 billion.

QUESTION

What was the occupation of most of the participants?

ANSWER

They had no area of specialty. Among others, geologists, mathematicians, consultants, graduate students, and military officers made submissions. They used tools from applied math, advanced physics, artificial intelligence, chaos theory, and other areas to analyze the data.

QUESTION

It is obvious that the GoldCorp story demonstrates the high-quality results that can be produced by collaboration from people with high levels of cognitive intelligence. Where is the emotional intelligence?

ANSWER

It comes from Rob McEwen. A person who understands others and can motivate them to be highly effective at bringing out the talents of people with high IQs.

COLLABORATION AT THE RIVER

Professors can use classroom exercises to help students understand how collaboration increases the exchange of ideas.

QUESTION

A man approaches a river. He must decide whether to swim upstream or downstream. What should he do?

ANSWER

He should determine the purpose of the swim. For exercise, he should swim upstream. For distance, downstream. If his goal is to cross the river, he should find a bridge.

QUESTION

What is the trap in the previous question?

ANSWER

If we do not broaden our horizon, we limit our options. Let's change the question and assign it to a group of students. The challenge? What group can be the most creative?

QUESTION

A man approaches a river. He must decide what to do next. How many choices can your group identify?

ANSWER

Students get creative when they collaborate:

- **Swims across the river.** Hit by a boat. Shot by border guards. Eaten by piranhas.
- **Swims upstream or downstream.** Gets lost. Drowns because he gets too tired to stay afloat. Goes over Niagara Falls.
- **Does not enter the water.** Misses a chance to cool down. Gets captured by the chasing police.

Occasionally, collaboration goes even further. Build a bridge. Collect tolls. Build condos. Dam up the river and generate electricity. Poison the river. Buy a boat and offer dinner cruises. Water ski. Ice skate. Connect to an aqueduct. Follow it to the source. Write a book.

GROUPTHINK

The story of collaboration would not be complete without mentioning the downside of collaboration. Groupthink is the behavior that occurs when people display pleasant or good-natured personal qualities in group decision making. Independent critical thinking and realistic appraisals of alternative courses of action become secondary to the group interaction. We think we have consensus when we simply have amiable behavior.

QUESTION

How serious is the danger of groupthink in decision making?

ANSWER

Researchers show that it is real. Starting as early as the 1950s, experiments show that forceful people with the wrong answer can convince others to conform.

SHILLER AND COLLABORATION

Robert Shiller, the Yale economist, saw the U.S. housing bubble that led to the 2008 financial crisis and was in a position to help avoid it. From 1990 to 2004, he served on an advisory panel for the Federal Reserve Bank of New York. This government agency could have raised interest rates, an act that might have halted the extreme rise in real estate prices.

QUESTION

Did Shiller warn the Federal Reserve Bank about the impending housing bubble that was the prime cause of the crisis?

ANSWER

Yes. Sort of. Shiller was quoted:

> I felt the need to use restraint. The consensus . . . was that there was no bubble and no need to raise interest rates. To suggest otherwise was distinctly uncomfortable. I [made my point] very gently, and felt vulnerable expressing such quirky views.

Shiller continued:

> Deviating too far from consensus leaves one feeling potentially ostracized from the group, with the risk that one may be terminated. (Robert J. Shiller, "Challenging the Crowd in Whispers, Not Shouts," *New York Times*, November 2, 2008)

Even a renowned economist of unquestioned stature on mistakes people make with their money succumbed to pressure to conform to his collaborators. Collaboration brings us the best ideas but the wrong collaboration can bury them in groupthink.

QUESTION

In 1961, the U.S. government supported the Bay of Pigs invasion of Cuba. The invasion plan was completely flawed yet it was "uncritically accepted" by advisors to President Kennedy. Why?

ANSWER

Groupthink was at work. The plan was filled with obviously false assumptions, including the ineffectiveness of Castro's air force, the weakness of Castro's army, and the inability of Castro to quell internal dissent. Senior advisors knew the reality but eventually ceased their objections to be part of the "team." The invasion was a disaster and subsequent findings showed a total groupthink process was at work.

QUESTION

Has the Cuba groupthink been repeated since 1961?

ANSWER

Many times. Consider the U.S. decision to invade Iraq in 2003 to uncover weapons of mass destruction that did not exist.

CONCLUSION AND FALLACIES

Collaboration produces results, particularly when accompanied by emotional intelligence and when care is take to avoid groupthink. Hence:

Fallacy 20. Understanding how to work with others is not an expected outcome of the liberal arts.
Reality 20. The liberal arts should embed collaboration without groupthink as a component of emotional intelligence.

Chapter Twenty-One

How Should Professors Handle Irrational Behavior? Why Do People Make Such Odd Decisions?

> The secret of life is honesty and fair dealing. If you can fake that, you've got it made.
>
> —Groucho Marx, American comedian

RATIONAL CHOICE THEORY

An economic theory claims people try to maximize their benefits and minimize their costs. Dan Ariely, a Duke University professor, disagrees. He claims we make choices comparing things that are easily comparable. Then we make predictably irrational decisions.

QUESTION

Why might a faculty advisor reject the dissertation draft?

ANSWER

The advisor may compare the work to other dissertations and conclude that it is not as good.

QUESTION

Dan Ariely told one group of one hundred students they needed a subscription to *The Economist*. They had three choices. Which did they pick?

- Online only: $59
- Print subscription: $125
- Print and online: $125

ANSWER

Eighty-four percent of the students took the print and online subscription. The remaining 16 percent took online only.

QUESTION

Ariely told a second group of one hundred students they needed a subscription. They had two choices. Which did they pick?

- Online only: $59
- Print and online: $125

ANSWER

The results were completely different. Sixty-eight percent took online only, and 32 percent took the print and online. The two experiments show people buy things in relation to other options.

QUESTION

Assume you are buying a new pen that costs twenty-five dollars. In the check-out line, someone tells you the pen is on sale for thirteen dollars in a store fifteen minutes away. Would you take the trip to buy the same pen and save twelve dollars?

ANSWER

Do not be surprised if many people say yes.

QUESTION

Change the situation and assume you were buying a new suit for $455. As you prepare to pay for it, someone tells you the suit is on sale for $443 in a store fifteen minutes away. Would you take the trip to buy the same suit and save $12?

ANSWER

Do not be surprised how quickly many people say no.

MARKET AND SOCIAL NORMS

The liberal arts should provide a conceptual framework for recognizing two approaches to decision making:

- **Social Norms.** People make friendly requests and interact in a community spirit.
- **Market Norms.** People seek value for their money and compare the benefits and the price.

QUESTION

Ariely cited a story where the American Association of Retired Persons (AARP) asked lawyers to help older people with legal problems. AARP agreed to pay thirty dollars an hour to one group. AARP asked other lawyers if they would do it for free. What was the result?

ANSWER

Few lawyers responded to thirty dollars an hour. It was not worth the money. This was a market norm. The free request was broadly accepted. The lawyers were willing to help those less fortunate. This was a social norm.

SOUTHWEST AIRLINES

Southwest Airlines had a policy of first-come, first-boarded. A person could log in online twenty-four hours in advance of departure and receive a boarding number. A low number offered the opportunity to choose many seats. A high number allowed boarding after many seats were taken. A Southwest fare could range from $119 to $314 on a flight from Hartford, Connecticut, to Fort Lauderdale, Florida. The high fare allowed boarding among the first fifteen passengers. Did many flyers take advantage of the higher fare?

ANSWER

No. Early boarding as a lottery was worthwhile, but paying to guarantee early boarding was not. Southwest boarding typically showed three to six people in slots one to fifteen. At sixteen, the line was filled with individuals who obtained a boarding pass online. People in spots sixteen to twenty-nine typically logged in during the first three seconds when boarding passes became available.

Update. Subsequently, Southwest changed the policy to allow individuals to pay an extra fifteen dollars per flight for the slots from sixteen to fifty-nine. The policy was an immediate success. Slots one to fifteen still had few takers.

PROCRASTINATION

Ariely points out that procrastination is the act of delaying completion of a task. He associates it with two categories.

- **Unimportant Tasks.** They are either too small to worry about or they interrupt more important tasks.
- **Important Uncontrollable Outcomes.** These are tasks where a person fears making a wrong choice with large consequences.

Ariely believes we can manage procrastination. He gave each of three classes different instructions for turning in three term papers.

- **Class A.** Choose deadlines with penalties for missing them. They could choose the last day of the class for all three papers.
- **Class B.** All papers due on last day of class.
- **Class C.** Papers due in the fourth, eighth, and twelfth weeks.

Subsequently, he compared the grades. They showed structure can reduce procrastination and improve performance.

- **Class A.** The group that chose its own deadlines had grades in the middle of the other two groups.
- **Class B.** The group where all papers were due on the last day of class had the worst grades.
- **Class C.** The group with three specific deadlines of the fourth, eighth, and twelfth weeks had the highest grades.

QUIRKY DECISIONS

The term "quirky" refers to something different, odd, or curious. Dan Ariely said people are quirky about the things they own. They do not make a correct assessment of value when they buy and sell.

- **Love of What We Have.** If we have something, we value it highly.
- **Focus on Loss, Not Gain.** If we exchange something, our perception of loss usually exceeds our perception of the gain.
- **Expectation of Others.** We think others should value things just as we do.

DUKE BASKETBALL GAME VALUE

Duke University gave basketball tickets to students two ways:

- **Camping Out.** Students could wait in line outside the ticket office. A limited number of tickets were issued on a first-come, first-served basis. Students camped for days through rain and sunshine.
- **Lottery.** A limited number of tickets were issued to students based upon a random drawing. The university had far more students than available tickets.

QUESTION

Dan Ariely called a student who did not win a ticket in the lottery. He offered to sell him a ticket and asked what price he would pay. How much do you think it was worth?

ANSWER

The student offered $175. A quote was, "The game would be exciting but $175 is a lot of money."

QUESTION

Ariely called a student who won a ticket after camping out for a week. He was asked at what price would he sell the ticket. What was the response?

ANSWER

The student said he would sell the ticket for $3,000. After negotiation, the lowest number was $2,400. A quote was, "Duke basketball is a large part of my life here."

COFFEE MUG OR CHOCOLATE?

Another valuation story occurred in an executive training seminar. The sponsor gave half of the attendees a coffee mug. The other half received a bar of Swiss chocolate. After everyone had a gift, the sponsor said anyone could exchange for the other item. What percentage do you think exchanged the gift?

ANSWER

The answer was **10 percent**. This is sometimes called the status quo trap. Once committed to ownership, people are reluctant to change.

TOO MANY CHOICES

Dan Ariely believes that too many choices distract us from achieving goals. Thus, people should simplify their world. This goes completely against human nature, which hates the elimination of alternatives.

QUESTION

An upscale grocery store allowed a professor to conduct an experiment using Wilkin & Sons exotic jams.

- On the first Saturday, shoppers passed a booth with a display of twenty-four different gourmet jams.
- One week later, the booth contained only six jams.

Researchers measured the percentage of people who stopped and tasted. They also measured the percent that bought. Which day produced the best results?

ANSWER

The day with six jams produced the most sales. With twenty-four choices, a higher percent stopped but few actually bought.

	Twenty-Four Choices	*Six Choices*
Percent who stopped	60	40
Percent who bought	3	30

IRRATIONAL EXPECTATIONS AND BEHAVIOR

Dan Ariely believes we lack the ability to let go of activities. We stay on committees that are a waste of time. We send holiday cards to people who have left our lives. Companies continue to sell products that no one wants.

Ariely also said expectations shape behavior in predictably irrational ways. If we expect an outcome, we think it happened. If fans of different sports teams watch a controversial play on the field, they interpret it differently even with multiple replays. Each expects its team to win.

QUESTION

College students were given a taste of two beers and then were offered a glass of the beer they preferred. Budweiser was one of the beers. The other was Budweiser with several drops of balsamic vinegar added to eight ounces. Which beer did they generally prefer?

ANSWER

It depended upon their expectation.

- Half of the students were not told about the vinegar. They chose the beer with the vinegar.
- The other half was told about the vinegar in advance. They mostly chose the Budweiser that did not have vinegar in it.

QUESTION

Continuing the beer experiment, a group of students was not told about the vinegar until after choosing the beer with vinegar in it. Did the knowledge after drinking the beer cause a negative reaction?

ANSWER

Nope. With subsequent knowledge, the students mostly liked the beer just as much as students who were never told about the vinegar.

LESSON LEARNED

Prior knowledge shapes expectations.

- If you tell people in advance that something will be distasteful, it will often meet their expectations.
- Subsequent knowledge merely informs.
- We cannot remove preconceptions and prior knowledge when making decisions.
- We can acknowledge that we are all biased.

LEVITT ON ECONOMICS

Now we switch to examine behavior when people make economic decisions. Steven Levitt, an economics professor, believes economists ignore conflicts that arise among three categories of incentives:

- **Economic.** Financial rewards or penalties.
- **Social.** Action or inaction to achieve recognition or avoid disapproval.
- **Moral.** An internal motivation to feel good about performing an ethical behavior or feel bad with a harmful act.

By ignoring these conflicts, Levitt argues we often fail to distinguish the difference between what is rational and what is not. He makes the following points:

- **Incentives.** The key to understanding behavior. Create the right incentives.
- **Conventional Wisdom.** Is often wrong. Think about it. Challenge it.
- **Causes and Effects.** Are hard to determine. How confident should we be that we know the cause of an event?
- **Self-Serving Behavior.** Drives actions.
- **Measurement.** To understand behavior, measure the right thing.

In his book *Freakonomics*, Levitt gives examples of how these factors shape decisions.

QUESTION

A house is for sale in a market where housing values range from $400,000 to $450,000. The low number is achievable in 30 days; the high number in 180 days. The real estate commission is 6 percent divided into four parts. The real estate companies representing the buyer and seller get 25 percent each. The buying and selling agents each get 25 percent. Does the selling agent have an incentive to hold out for the top price?

ANSWER

No. The agent gets $750 more commission at the higher price but can sell the house in one month. She can use the next five months to make sales that can net $6,000 a month.

	Price	*Commission*	*Agent Share*
In one month	400,000	24,000	6,000
In six months	450,000	27,000	6,750

QUESTION

A blood bank sought to increase donations of blood. It offered ten dollars to anyone who donated blood. The impact was a decrease in the level of donations. What happened?

ANSWER

An economic incentive replaced a moral incentive. Instead of being praised for a good act, people got a small amount of money. The praise was worth more than ten dollars.

QUESTION

Continuing the previous exercise. What would result if the economic incentive was $1,000 instead of $10?

ANSWER

Donations may rise at $1,000 but so would bad behavior. The blood bank could experience theft of blood. People could try to sell counterfeit blood, perhaps from pigs. Ineligible donors could present fake identification papers.

Note: Levitt quotes W. C. Fields who said, "A thing worth having is worth cheating for."

QUESTION

Levitt describes a day care center where parents had to pick up children by 4:00 pm. Ten percent of parents were late by fifteen or more minutes. The center imposed a fine of three dollars a day. What happened after imposition of the fine?

ANSWER

The percent of lateness jumped from 10 to 25 percent.

QUESTION

After a few months, the day care center ended the fine. What happened?

ANSWER

Lateness stayed at 25 percent as a financial incentive replaced a moral incentive. At three dollars, the fine was too small. It was a bargain compared to the cost of day care. The fine showed lateness was not painful to the day care center.

FEAR OVERCOMES THE ODDS

We should not leave irrational decision making without pointing out a lesson from Nassim Taleb about decision-making odds. It is not irrational to ignore the odds when the fear of a large loss is part of the calculation.

QUESTION

Suppose we offer someone the opportunity to remove a ball from a jar containing one hundred balls without seeing the color. The jar has one hundred white balls and one black ball. If a white ball is selected, the person receives $200. If a black ball is selected, the person will pay $8,000. Is this a good wager?

ANSWER

Taleb points out that this is unacceptable for most people. The loss of $8,000 is not justified by the opportunity to win $200. The probability is not the point. The magnitude of the loss makes the bet too dangerous to accept.

QUESTION

An insurance company is exposed to losses from homes it insures against hurricanes in Florida. It offers an investor the right to invest $10,000 at 16 percent interest for three years. At the time, competing rates are 4 percent.

The money will be kept in an account at a major bank and the insurance company will return the money with interest. Why would an insurer pay such a high rate of interest?

ANSWER

This is a catastrophe bond ("Cat" bond). The agreement contains a clause that the money would be used to cover insured losses if a hurricane struck Florida. The investor could lose the entire principal and interest.

QUESTION

Would anyone accept the exposure in the previous example of a "Cat" bond?

ANSWER

It is a good bet in terms of probability. A hurricane might cause damage in Florida once every ten to fifteen years. The benefit is worth the risk. At the same time, the individual is not likely to invest his life savings. Instead, one investment in Florida hurricanes, another for California earthquakes, one more for Nebraska tornadoes, and fifteen others on natural disasters could be profitably spread over a portfolio of events. The point is one large event that could bankrupt us is unacceptable even though statistically it is a good opportunity.

LESSONS FOR THE LIBERAL ARTS

With respect to rational and irrational behavior, we can draw lessons.

- **Ariely.** Individuals and organizations do not easily acknowledge they are often irrational. This is true even when presented with evidence to the contrary.
- **Levitt.** We should not limit ourselves to quantitative tools to understand relationships in economics. Causation can be elusive.
- **Taleb.** The full story is not told by the odds of gain or loss. The position of the decision maker affects the validity of the reasoning process.

CONCLUSION AND FALLACIES

One of the most useful developmental skills for college students is to distinguish between rational and irrational behavior. This is particularly critical as high school years are often filled with situations that seem to be illogical on the face of them. Young people need to mature and a liberal arts exposure helps in the development. Hence:

Fallacy 21. Liberal arts encourage students to avoid irrational behavior.
Reality 21. Liberal arts should help students understand and deal with irrational behavior.

Chapter Twenty-Two

How Does It All Come Together? What Do We Know at the End of Our Journey?

> If you don't know where you're going, you'll end up someplace else.
>
> —Yogi Berra, American baseball player

We started with the story of six blind men who were asked to describe an elephant after touching different parts of its body. In a similar way, we are now finished touching the corpus of the liberal arts. What conclusions might we draw?

COMPONENTS OF THE LIBERAL ARTS

The different parts of the liberal arts can be broadly identified by category.

Environment of Learning

- **Economics.** Who is willing to pay for an education?
- **Philosophy.** What does it mean to be an educated person?
- **Politics.** What should be included given a diversity of individuals seeking different outcomes.

Construct of Learning

- **Cognitive Component.** The content that is learned about facts and beliefs.
- **Emotional Component.** The assumptions, opinions, biases, and psychological facilitators and impediments to learning.

Structure of Learning

- **Curriculum.** What is the subject matter to be covered?
- **Subject Matter Content.** What readings and other materials will be used?
- **Delivery.** How will knowledge be transferred?
- **Conclusion.** When will the desired state be attained for individuals?

People of Learning

- **Credentials.** What do faculty members and staff need as academic qualifications?
- **Motivation.** Do the people want to help others learn?
- **Personal Characteristics.** Are the people capable of playing on the team?

QUESTION

What can we do about the environment?

ANSWER

This is the subject for another book on another day.

QUESTION

How about the construct of learning?

ANSWER

We already covered this. Add emotional intelligence to intellectual quotient as a selection process for faculty. Reward teachers instead of researchers when individuals are hired primarily to be instructors. Reward people who facilitate learning.

QUESTION

How about the structure of learning?

ANSWER

Mold the curriculum as a combination of liberal arts for the breadth of knowledge and upper-division majors for the depth of knowledge in an area needed in the modern world. Align the two parts with appropriate subject matter content so critical thinking leads to decision making and action. Use technology and learning methods that encourage the creation and retention of valued knowledge and behaviors.

QUESTION

How about the people of learning?

ANSWER

Determine that they have background experience and academic credentials to cover the IQ component of courses they teach. Assess their attitudes and motivations for the proper orientation to learning. Answer honestly the question, "Do I like this person?" If all three are positive, pay the person a reasonable wage and get out of their way.

QUESTION

Is there any viable way that needed reforms will take place?

ANSWER

Maybe. We do have the Association of American Colleges and Universities (AACU) and Southern New Hampshire University as models to consider and Nicholas Lemann for an intellectual structure.

ASSOCIATION OF AMERICAN COLLEGES AND UNIVERSITIES GENERAL EDUCATION OUTCOMES

The first two years of college generally require a program of general education. This is the common cultural heritage so revered by a properly offered introduction to the liberal arts.

Professors largely agree on the concept of general education but disagree on what it should include. Couched in scholarly terms and confronted by powerful elements of the faculty, even the slightest reforms get bogged down in absurd arguments and trivial accusations.

Outside forces and sponsors are weighing in. A major revision was proposed by the AACU. It created tools to measure sixteen learning outcomes in three categories:

- **Cognitive and Practical Skills**
- **Personal and Social Responsibility**
- **Integrative and Applied Learning**

Not much progress has been made aligning individual college curricula with the AACU outcomes.

SOUTHERN NEW HAMPSHIRE UNIVERSITY

The answer to reform may start from the ground up in terms of structure and the top down in terms of college boards and presidents. In 2003, Southern New Hampshire University was a minor school offering culinary arts, business, and criminal justice programs to some twenty-five hundred students. It was a modest success. The president and faculty recognized technology and social trends were changing the landscape for higher education. The school developed and delivered distance learning in the right context of offerings. By 2017, more than fifteen thousand students were enrolled in one hundred graduate, undergraduate, and specialty-skill programs. It still had fewer than three thousand students registered on campus.

LEMANN ON GENERAL EDUCATION

Nicholas Lemann, a Columbia University professor, argues for a liberal arts curriculum mostly for students with intellectual capacity and solid writing and math skills. Courses cover how we take positions, draw conclusions, and explain our beliefs to others. What makes a compelling argument? To achieve this liberal arts foundation, he proposed eight courses.

- Information Acquisition
- Cause and Effect
- Interpretation of Written Meaning

- Numerical Literacy
- Personal Perspectives
- Visual Language
- Thinking in Time
- Argumentation

CONCLUSION AND FALLACIES

Thus, it all comes together. The liberal arts foundation of colleges and universities is likely the most convincing explanation of the success of Western society. It is being eroded by a failure to make reforms. We know what needs to be done. Do we have the strength of character to do it? Hence:

Fallacy 22. The liberal arts are responding well to the challenges of today.
Reality 22. The liberal arts are in the doldrums and we need to take steps to revive them.

Index

About the Author

John J. Hampton is a professor of business at St. Peter's University in New Jersey. In a faculty capacity, he was an endowed chair holder twice, department chair, director of a division of research, and director of graduate business programs. He was the dean of the schools of business at Seton Hall and Connecticut State universities and evening school at Saint Peter's. He was provost of the College of Insurance and State University of New York Maritime College, both in New York City.

Jack is the author of more than thirty books, two of which were recognized with innovation awards (2008 and 2012). The latter book was also selected by the American Library Association as one of three outstanding business reference books. His earlier book on higher education, *Culture, Intricacies, and Obsessions in Academia: Why Colleges and Universities are Struggling to Deliver the Goods*, was published by Rowman & Littlefield in 2017.

CPSIA information can be obtained
at www.ICGtesting.com
Printed in the USA
BVOW03s0342090917
494187BV00007B/9/P

9 781475 837964